TYPES, SHADOWS, AND CASSERLES

TYPES, SHADOWS, AND CASSERLES

FINDING CHRIST
IN YOUR DAILY LIFE

WHITNEY OWENS HEMSATH

ZERAPHIM PRESS

Published by Zeraphim Press.
Provo, UT.

© 2024 by Whitney Owens Hemsath.
www.whitneyhemsath.com.

Cover and interior design by Emily Strong Rogers.
Edited by Jeanna Stay.
All photos are courtesy of Whitney Hemsath unless otherwise credited.
Icon images courtesy of Flaticon.com.

ISBN 978-1-963659-00-9 (paperback)
ISBN 978-1-963659-01-6 (hardcover)
ISBN 978-1-963659-02-3 (ebook)

TO MY ETERNAL BEST FRIEND DUSTIN,
WHOSE UNFAILING LOVE AND SUPPORT MAKE HIM
MY FAVORITE TYPE AND SHADOW OF CHRIST

CONTENTS

INTRODUCTION

When I was a newlywed, I had the honor of teaching seminary and would often play a game with my seminary students. They could name any object, and I had to come up with how that object was like Christ or reminded us of Him. Then I'd give them an object, and they had to do the same.

Some objects were easy: Christ is like a puppy because He is loyal to you and loves you even if you've been mean to Him; pillows remind us of Christ because He comforts us, and in Him, we can find rest.

Other things were more challenging, though, like a flat tire. But the trickiest ones usually proved to be the most profound. As a class, we realized that a flat tire symbolizes a need to change. Whether that need for change is provoked by the "wear and tear" of life or by running into something hazardous, making the change is impossible if you don't have the right tools and someone else to teach you how. Therefore, a flat tire reminds us that when we need to change, we need to let the Savior help us, and we need to use the gospel tools He's given us. If we don't, we'll never be able to get back on the road and reach our destination.

The more I played the game with my students, the more I saw this pattern of Christ woven throughout the tapestry of my life. I could look back and see gospel lessons not just in the monumental moments but in the mundane as well. That year, I even found Him in a poorly prepared lasagna (you can look forward to reading about that culinary disaster in chapter 1).

I was eventually called as a Gospel Doctrine teacher, and even though I wasn't teaching seminary anymore, I continued to challenge myself to find Christ in my everyday life. Over time, I recorded those moments and insights, intending to turn them into a book.

Then one Sunday, a sister came to me after one of my lessons and said, "I wish I could tie things into the gospel like you can, but my brain just doesn't work like that."

It broke my heart that she felt that way, but her confession prompted me to ask around, and I realized she wasn't alone. I conducted an informal poll on social media to a group of LDS moms, asking how they would describe their ability to find symbols of Christ in the world around them. Fifty-eight percent of participants responded, "I struggle. I hear others discuss their scriptural insights and think *How are you doing that?*"

That's when I knew I needed to change the goal for the book I'd started writing. It needed to include not only my experiences and insights but also a guide to show people how to find their own insights and see symbols of Christ in their lives.

Taking an event from my life and tying it into the gospel has always come easily to me. I'd never stopped to think about how I was doing it, let alone how I could teach someone else to do it. However, once I took a moment to truly ponder, the Spirit opened my understanding and helped me break down my mental process into three simple steps I believe anyone can follow:

1. Pick the Players
2. Dig for Details
3. Match to the Master

I'll explain each step in its own chapter, but please know that my process is not by any means the only way to find Christ in all things. It is simply a way that works for me, and I hope it will be helpful to you.

While the ability to find Christ in all things might come naturally to some as a spiritual gift, I believe it is a gift anyone can work toward developing. After all, the Savior Himself promised, "Ask, and it shall be given you; seek, and ye shall find" (Matthew 7:7).

My hope is that as you ask for this gift and actively seek it by following these steps, you'll develop your own testimony that everything we encounter is an object lesson waiting to happen, waiting to point our souls toward Him. It isn't a matter of knowing where to look; it's simply a matter of training ourselves to see.

EVERYDAY SYMBOLS

"All things are created and made to bear record of me, both things which are temporal, and things which are spiritual; things which are in the heavens above, and things which are on the earth, and things which are in the earth, and things which are under the earth, both above and beneath: all things bear record of me."

MOSES 6:63

IN A 9×13 PAN

When it comes to everyday things, nothing fits that description in my mind quite so much as cooking. As a mother of four, I cook meal after meal, day after day, week after week. And while I might not be the best cook, I can at least follow a recipe—in theory.

To me, recipes are like the pirate's code; they're more a set of guidelines than actual rules. While I'd like to claim that my frequent deviations from recipes are rooted in some artistic expression of culinary creativity, the truth is that they're usually because I don't have everything the recipe calls for, and I'm either too tired or too broke to run to the store for the exact ingredients. Instead, I try to make it work with the food I have on hand.

My favorite type of food to apply this *make-it-work* cooking style to is casseroles. They're so forgiving. I've learned that as long as I have a good ratio of sauce to stuff (see how technical my kitchen skills are?) and melt enough cheese on top, I can almost always make any casserole work. If I don't have pasta, I can use rice. If I don't have enough rice, I can add more veggies to bulk it up. If I don't have sour cream, I can use cream of whatever soup or Greek yogurt. As long as the sauce-to-stuff ratio is good, I can take leftover tomato sauce or canned beans that would've gone bad in my fridge, toss them in with everything else, and transform them into something wonderful my family will eat and enjoy.

Sometimes, though, even when I do have all the right ingredients in the right quantities, I still have to get creative. Take, for example, the first time I made lasagna for my husband.

As a newlywed, I was working full-time, taking two graduate-level courses, and serving as an early-morning seminary teacher. The few hours I had at home in the evenings were precious, and this particular night I had just spent one of those hours thawing beef and browning it, thawing frozen spinach and draining it, wrangling our can opener to work on the spaghetti sauce, and grating a pound of mozzarella—all in the world's narrowest excuse for an apartment kitchen.

Finally, it was time to layer. The noodles went on the bottom, then the meat sauce, then the cottage cheese and spinach, then some mozzarella. I repeated all the layers, topped it off with the rest of the cheese, and stood back to admire my creation.

It looked beautiful, just how I remembered making it with my mom. This spinach lasagna recipe had been her signature dish. It was what she fed the missionaries any time we had them over for dinner, and it was always a crowd pleaser.

Anxious to get the cheese bubbling and amaze my new husband with my domestic dexterity, I put the lasagna in the oven, but I didn't remember how long it needed to bake for. I checked the pasta box for the recommended time, expecting to see something like 30–45 minutes. When I saw the words *8–10 minutes*, I was thoroughly confused

I was even more confused when I saw the word *boil* that preceded them. Who boils lasagna noodles?

Apparently everyone but my mother. After a confused and frantic phone call to my sweet mom, I learned that two types of lasagna noodles exist in this world—the no-boil ones my mother special ordered for years, which were the only kind I had ever seen used, and the cheaper, more common ones found in abundance at my grocery store that must be cooked prior to assembling one's lasagna.

By the time I learned this very important lesson, it was already 7:30 at night. My poor crunchy noodles were buried under layers of sauce, meat, spinach, and cheese. I had no idea what to do. Disassembling the lasagna was not an option.

Neither was discarding it. The ingredients for the lasagna hadn't been cheap and our budget was tight. My husband would be home from class soon, feeling famished, and I needed to find a way to salvage the meal.

Relying heavily on my sauce-to-stuff ratio, I poured some extra watered-down tomato sauce around the edges, reduced the oven temperature, and added an extra 15 minutes to the timer. With a prayer, I put my runny experiment into the oven.

I don't remember how long I had to leave it in there, but I do remember that by the time we ate that night, we were yawning between bites. The top layer of noodles was overcooked and only made palatable by the abundance of cheese broiled on top, but the bottom layers had eventually cooked just right and tasted great. It didn't turn out the way I'd wanted it to, but despite my shortcomings, it still wound up being edible and (mostly) enjoyable.

TYPES, SHADOWS, AND CASSEROLES

The prophet Alma taught that "all things denote there is a God" (Alma 30:44), and my culinary catastrophe is no exception. When I took the time to ponder the symbolism in this event, I realized that if I try to do things on my own by leaning unto my own understanding (Proverbs 3:5), I'm bound to fail. But just as the noodle makers provided clear instructions on the lasagna box to guide me through making a successful lasagna, my Eternal Maker has provided clear instructions in the scriptures and through His prophets to guide me through living a successful life.

Following those instructions can prevent a lot of heartache and stress, but even when I mess up, hope isn't lost. I can always repent and fix things because, just like a casserole, Christ is very forgiving. It doesn't mean there won't be consequences for my mistakes (remember that hard-to-eat top layer of noodles?). But no matter where I'm at in life, what weaknesses I have, or which mistakes I've made, if I add enough Christ to my life and give myself enough time, I'll turn out okay.

Some people might think it's silly to find Christ in a casserole. (Others might think it's silly to even consider lasagna a casserole.) But I've learned we truly can find Christ in *all* things.

Every symbol of every aspect of the law was about Christ.

In the Year of the Lasagna, I had the privilege of teaching and studying the Old Testament with my seminary students. While we did our best to delve into the law of Moses, I won't pretend that we became experts on all its details. I've taught the Old Testament in Sunday School, taken institute classes on it, and read it cover to cover—and I *still* can't remember the difference between a heave offering and a peace offering. So, if the phrases "Mosaic law" and "Old Testament" make your brain want to shut off, I get it.

But even if I and my little band of groggy-eyed students didn't understand everything about the law of Moses, we did learn what the law was all about. If you take nothing else from this book, please know that every symbol of every aspect of the law was about Christ. The prophet Abinadi taught this, though he didn't use the word *symbol*. Instead, he said everything in the law of Moses was a "type" (Mosiah 13:31) and a "shadow" (Mosiah 16:14) of Christ's Atonement yet to come.

What exactly are types and shadows? A type is someone or something that shares the defining characteristics of another person or thing. For example, oranges and grapes, though different from each other in many ways, are still both types of fruit. They both share the defining characteristics of fruit: they have seeds surrounded by an edible flesh that grew from a flower.

A shadow, in the scriptural context, means something that bears the form or likeness of something else, often something yet to come. This is similar to the literary term *foreshadowing*—the idea that what we see now resembles, in some degree, what will follow.

To illustrate how everything in the law of Moses is a type and a shadow of Christ, let's imagine what a day in your life might have looked like if you were an ancient Israelite in Moses's times.

A DAY IN THE LIFE

The afternoon heat penetrates your family's tent. You aren't looking forward to the trek across camp to the well, but your family needs extra water for washing because they are ceremonially unclean after helping a sick neighbor. A new day with its fresh, clean status begins for your spouse and children at sundown but only if you can get enough water to wash their clothes before then.

You go to retrieve your two clay vessels but notice, with a tinge of panic, that someone left them uncovered. The first one is dry and empty, but as you peer into the second, your heart sinks. There, floating in a few inches of water, is a dead bug.

Knowing what must be done, you sigh and take the jug outside. You lift it high, then thrust it down. The dust muffles the tinkling sounds of shattering ceramic.

Having complied with the law, you swallow to wet your parched mouth, fetch the remaining vessel, and begin the long walk to the well—a trip you must now make twice as many times.

BREAKING DOWN THE BROKEN POT

If you're like me, it's hard to read the above example without immense gratitude for indoor plumbing—I feel so blessed to turn on a tap and have water on demand! In addition to gratitude, though, chances are you also had a feeling that smashing the jug over one dead insect was extreme and wasteful.

Yet that's exactly what the law of Moses demanded. After listing the various animals considered unclean, which included all non-locust insects, the Lord told Israel,

> These are unclean to you among all that creep: whosoever doth touch them, when they be dead, shall be unclean until the even.
>
> And upon whatsoever any of them, when they are dead, doth fall, it shall be unclean; whether it be any vessel of wood, or raiment, or skin, or sack, whatsoever vessel it be, wherein any work is done, it must be put into water, and it shall be unclean until the even; so it shall be cleansed.

And every earthen vessel, whereinto any of them falleth, whatsoever is in it shall be unclean; and ye shall break it. (Leviticus 11:31–33, emphasis added)

Yes, really, a dead bug inside a clay pot meant they had to destroy the whole vessel.

But only if it was clay; verse thirty-two said wood or leather containers could simply be washed. It seems like an odd double standard, doesn't it? In fact, when I first read about the law of Moses, all its rules and restrictions seemed arbitrary, serving only to test ancient Israel's obedience to God.

However, the more I studied the law in preparation for my seminary lessons, the more I realized it wasn't about blind obedience. As Jacob put it, the law was about "pointing our souls to [Christ]" (Jacob 4:5).

The prophet Alma summed up the law's purpose, stating, "And behold, this is the whole meaning of the law, every whit pointing to that great and last sacrifice; and that great and last sacrifice will be the Son of God, yea, infinite and eternal" (Alma 34:14).

I love that Alma didn't just say that the Mosaic law pointed the souls of God's covenant people toward the Savior; he said *every whit*—meaning every tiny part—of the law was meant to point them toward His sacrifice. Even the rule about smashing tainted clay jugs while merely washing wooden ones pointed to Christ. But how?

Unclean things, as spelled out in the law, were symbolic of sin. They represented mortal imperfections, things that could keep us from approaching the throne of God and becoming like

Him. This is the symbolic foundation to understanding much of the law of Moses.

But what about the different treatment for vessels made of different materials? The answer lies in considering what material *we* are made of. In Genesis 2:7, we read, "And the Lord God formed man of the dust of the ground, and breathed into his nostrils the breath of life; and man became a living soul."

We are not made of wood or leather. We are those who "dwell in houses of clay, whose foundation is in the dust" (Job 4:19). We are earthen vessels.

Understanding that symbolism, can you now imagine the impact of smashing those clay containers whenever they were tainted with even the smallest unclean thing? Can you imagine hearing the shattering crash as one hit the ground and surveying the irreparable mess of shards lying in the dirt?

What a powerful, tangible lesson that the tiniest sin still leaves us broken. What a great visual to show that when we die, we return to the dust of the earth—useless and wasted in our broken state. Every time a pot was destroyed, it was meant to inspire a longing for redemption, a hope for someone or something to save them from such permanent destruction.

It was meant to point their souls to Christ.

EVERY DAY, IN EVERY DISPENSATION

This example of the poignant imagery contained in the law of Moses (and there are many more examples like it) is often overlooked. In many of the classes I've attended at church, lessons on Mosaic law seem to focus only on the tabernacle or various

**God intends
for His people
to learn of Him
not only on the
Sabbath or in
His holy house
but everywhere,
every day.**

types of sacrifices. I realize this is usually due to time constraints and the teacher's desire to focus on the seemingly bigger symbols, but while the tabernacle and sacrifices are indeed rich with parallels, it's important to realize that the Lord, in His wisdom, did not confine this beautiful Messiah-centered symbolism to religious places and rituals. Instead, He embedded these symbolic reminders into every aspect of ancient Israel's lives, from cooking food to lending money, from getting sick to giving birth. God intended for His people to learn of Him not only on the Sabbath or in His holy house but everywhere, every day.

It is for this reason that Paul, after Christ's Resurrection, described the law as a "schoolmaster to bring us unto Christ" (Galatians 3:24). The Lord didn't want His people to remember Him only every so often. Theirs was a daily, ever-present spiritual education through a world filled with symbols of the Savior, and ours can be too.

I say *can be* because learning is a choice. Just because someone is teaching doesn't mean the class is paying attention.

Some Israelites did learn from their Mosaic law schoolmaster. After lamenting "my strength faileth because of mine iniquity," the Psalmist observed, "I am like a broken vessel" (Psalm 31:10, 12). The Israelites who fled to the Americas clearly understood that the law was meant to point us to Christ (see the previously quoted scriptures in Jacob 4:5 and Alma 34:14).

Other Israelites, however, didn't learn. They didn't pay attention to their schoolmaster. They were the rowdy students in the back, or the ones busy passing notes or gossiping, or even the ones staring out the window, longing to be somewhere else.

The Lord Himself described them as "a rebellious house, which have eyes to see, and see not" (Ezekiel 12:2). They were blind to the daily lessons available to them, and theirs was a voluntary blindness.

As easy as it is at times to dismiss the ancient Israelites as spiritually inferior and quick to forget, we should be careful how we judge them. While the law of Moses has been fulfilled, it isn't proof that we've evolved as a chosen people. We are not immune to any of the stiff-neckedness or weak faith we read about as Israel wandered in the wilderness.

I have never coveted my neighbor's wife, but there have been times when I've coveted how quickly my neighbor's wife lost all her baby weight compared to me. I have never bowed to a golden calf, but I've had moments of worshiping the idol of financial security, like when I haven't paid as generous a fast offering as I knew I could.

There have also been many days I've taken a pharisaical approach to scripture study. I'm not talking about the days I only had a widow's mite of time or energy to dedicate to scripture study; sometimes a quick verse at night is truly all we can do, and the Lord does not condemn us for it (Luke 21:1–4). I'm talking about the days I had time to binge my favorite shows and scroll aimlessly on my phone, yet when it came time for the scriptures, I merely skimmed through a verse or chapter in hopes of attaining some imaginary check mark of obedience, all while neglecting "the weightier matters"—the *why* of scripture study (Matthew 23:23). I may have read the scriptures, but I had failed to "write them upon the table of [my] heart" (Proverbs 7:3).

I don't point out these examples to make anyone feel discouraged or chastised, simply to illustrate that we in the latter days are just as mortal and prone to sin as ancient Israel was.

Where, then, is our schoolmaster? Our prevalence of daily reminders? Our ever-present symbolism? If God is unchanging and He filled ancient Israel's lives with object lessons to lovingly and consistently direct them back to Him, wouldn't He do the same with our lives as well?

I testify that He does. Everything we see and experience in this world that Christ created has the power to serve as a reminder of Him and His divinity as well as teach us about our relationship to Him.

The prophet Nephi likewise testified, "All things which have been given of God from the beginning of the world, unto man, are the typifying of [Christ]" (2 Nephi 11:4). Note that he doesn't say all things which have been given of God *to Moses* or all things given unto humanity *since the days of Sinai*. No, he says that from the beginning of the world, *all* things that humanity has received from God are types of Christ.

That includes all things in our lives right now.

ETERNAL BENEFITS

"For thou blessest, O Lord, and it shall be blessed
for ever."

1 CHRONICLES 17:27

DEFINING *ETERNAL*

In the following chapters, we'll discuss how to practice finding
Christ in all things. The process will include asking questions,
writing lists, making charts, researching definitions, and more.
The more we understand the eternal nature of the benefits that
come from training our brains to find Christ in all things, the
more likely we are to implement the practice. So to begin deepening our understanding, let's look at the word *eternal*.

We often associate eternal with things yet to come. For
example, eternal life is something we achieve only after we've

died and been resurrected, and when we say something will happen "in the eternities," we think of it happening sometime far away in the future. Even the phrase "eternal companion" evokes the idea that they are our companion from that moment forward, for the rest of time.

> **Finding Christ in all things benefits our future, present, *and* past.**

The concept of eternity, however, is not just about the future. The word *eternal* means "lasting or existing forever; without end *or beginning*" (definition from Oxford Languages, emphasis added). It would serve us well to think of the eternal benefits of finding Christ in all things as they pertain not only to our future but also to our present and past.

LOOKING TO THE PAST

Perhaps one of the most profound ways developing this practice relates to the past is in our ability to find deeper meaning and more personal applications in the scriptures—the words of the people and prophets who came before us. Finding Christ in all things is an exercise in finding and interpreting symbols, and the scriptures are rife with symbolism to be found and interpreted.

As you read through the scriptures, some passages (especially those with visions and dreams) will clearly be symbolic; they make no sense as literal accounts. But even passages that are histories of events that actually occurred, such as the stories of David and Goliath or Lehi dwelling in a tent, can be filled with spiritual insights when treated symbolically.

Taking literal scriptural accounts and finding symbolic meaning in them is what Nephi referred to as likening the scriptures unto ourselves. In fact, Nephi even specified that this likening practice was not to be done only with the overtly symbolic passages, but rather *all* scriptural passages. "For I did liken *all* scriptures unto us, that it might be for our profit and learning" (1 Nephi 19:23, emphasis added).

Our understanding of the scriptures will deepen and our testimonies will be fortified as we learn the art of interpreting symbols and likening them to ourselves.

LOOKING TO YOUR PERSONAL PAST

Another way this practice of finding Christ in all things can relate to the past is in its ability to help us view prior events in our life with a new perspective, potentially even healing old wounds.

During my mission I had a companion who I'll call Hermana. Hermana and I were not exactly best friends. As my senior companion, she dictated what I could do in lessons, which was almost always limited to reading a single scripture aloud. She called me prideful and ignorant yet refused to do companionship study with me. My opinions about our investigators were irrelevant to her. I spent many nights crying myself to sleep.

We had one particular investigator who I'll call Abuelo. He was the elderly father of a member who had recently returned to church. They were both wonderful people, but it was hard to tell how interested Abuelo was in the gospel because he rarely spoke. He would usually only nod or shake his head to answer any questions Hermana asked. He also couldn't read, so we knew he wasn't studying the scriptures on his own between our lessons.

Literacy and a chatty disposition are by no means requirements for baptism, but not having either of those things does make it challenging to ensure someone is prepared to make sacred covenants. Not impossible but challenging. However, instead of taking the time to really work with Abuelo, my companion seemed determined to rush him into baptism as soon as possible, a mere two weeks after we had first started teaching him.

I was certain he wasn't prepared. It seemed to me he didn't understand many of the doctrines and was simply nodding when Hermana prompted him to. She pushed forward with the baptism though, and it came as no surprise to me that when it was time for Abuelo's baptismal interview, he was in there for a very long time. The missionaries conducting the interview finally came out and lectured us about how woefully unready Abuelo was and how they had to practically reteach him everything.

I was embarrassed. This was not the kind of missionary I wanted to be seen as. (Okay, so maybe Hermana was right about me having a bit of pride.) But while the elders had their reservations, between their lengthy reteachings and Hermana's persuading, they did finally approve Abuelo for baptism as long as he came to church a second time.

With my concerns ignored, I felt like there was nothing I could do but tag along as Hermana continued planning his baptism. She arranged for it to happen immediately after church that coming Sunday, as soon as Abuelo had met the requirement of attending sacrament meeting twice.

Since neither of us could perform the baptism, Hermana asked a new sixteen-year-old priest in the ward to do the honors, and he was excited. Sunday came, Abuelo showed up to church, and as soon as the meetings were over, we gathered by the font. Old Abuelo staggered into the water. The young priest gripped Abuelo's wrist with one hand and raised his other in the air. He said the words of the ordinance, then tried to lower Abuelo into the water.

But Abuelo wouldn't go.

Not because he didn't want to. He simply didn't know how. We had rushed the process so much that we never rehearsed the actual motions of sitting down and leaning back to help immerse himself into the water-filled font.

We tried to verbally coach him through the process, and the priest finally got Abuelo partially under. But he wasn't fully immersed. He didn't get fully immersed on the second try either.

Or the third.

Or the fourth.

At that point, I was not the only one embarrassed. I could see it in Abuelo's face. He was frustrated. So were the young priest and all the attendees. I was so mad at Hermana for rushing this process and hurrying someone into the font who wasn't ready. I was afraid that Abuelo would quit and leave and never come back because of the embarrassment.

A senior missionary came to our rescue. He took off his suit coat and shoes, grabbed a chair from a classroom, and climbed into the font in his Sunday clothes. He put the chair on the floor of the font, helped Abuelo sit in it, and held Abuelo's feet under the water while the young priest tipped the chair back.

It took a total of six tries, two men, a chair, and numberless silent prayers, but Abuelo was finally baptized by immersion. Any relief the eventual success brought me, however, was eclipsed by my embarrassment and the resentment I harbored toward my companion.

I went on to have other companions I got along with much better. I transferred to areas where no one knew me as the missionary who forgot to adequately prepare someone for baptism. Thankfully, I was able to see other investigators enter the waters of baptism (and be successfully immersed on the first try because I made sure we rehearsed the physical motions with them). But for more than a decade after Abuelo's baptism, I felt bitter toward Hermana every time I thought about the experience—until I tried to find Christ in it.

By searching for symbols of Christ in what had happened, I began to see Abuelo's baptism as not just a painful memory or a cautionary tale. It also became a symbol of my own relationship with Christ. I realized that every time I mix up my priorities and focus on what I think will make me look good instead of focusing on those things that will make me spiritually prepared, I become just like Hermana. When I considered the font as if it were mortality, I also saw myself in Abuelo, having to continually suffer the consequences of those mixed-up priorities.

Whatever you need to succeed, no matter how unconventional, Christ will provide it. He will do whatever it takes, for however long it takes, to help you.

Most importantly though, I realized that no matter how many times I feel like I just can't get things right, since I'm still in the font—still in mortality—I still have time to try again, and I don't have to try alone. Just as the senior elder climbed into the font with Abuelo, the Savior is willing to enter my life and hold me as I try and try again. Whatever I need to succeed, no matter how unconventional, I know Christ will provide it. If it means sticking a chair in the font, so be it. He will do whatever it takes, for however long it takes, to help me.

As I used this process to find Christ in all things, the story that haunted me with bitterness for over a decade became a precious reminder of Christ's unfailing love and patience. How could I continue to harbor ill feelings toward a companion who provided me with such a treasure? I couldn't. While nothing can change the events of the past, finding Christ in all things helped me soften my heart, change my perspective of the past, and heal an old wound I had let fester for far too long.

A PRESENT FOR OURSELVES

In addition to helping us better understand and heal from the past, the eternal benefits of finding Christ in all things also strengthen us in the present.

No matter how strong we think we currently are, we can't rely solely on past spiritual experiences to sustain us in the future. We need as many new spiritual experiences as we can get, every day. Some spiritual experiences are easier to facilitate; we rarely struggle to remember Christ when we go to the temple, say our prayers, or study our scriptures. However, we can't spend every moment doing those things. Life demands that at some point we get up off our knees, close the Gospel Library app, and take care of the demands of mortality. When we do, Satan is ready with every tool in his arsenal to distract us and lure us away from Christ, and it can happen so much faster than we'd like to think.

Take, for example, the ancient Israelites in Jerusalem just before they were taken into captivity. Jeremiah was their prophet (he was a contemporary of Lehi), and the people felt the pressure of Babylon approaching. They considered fleeing to Egypt to seek protection from Babylon, but before deciding anything, the people turned to Jeremiah and asked him to consult the Lord to know what they should do. Their faith in the Lord and in Jeremiah was inspiring. Despite the threat of captivity looming large, they said to Jeremiah, "Whether it be good, or whether it be evil, we will obey the voice of the Lord our God, to whom we send thee; that it may be well with us, when we obey the voice of the Lord our God" (Jeremiah 42:6).

Jeremiah obliged, asked the Lord, and the Lord waited ten days to reply (Jeremiah 42:7). During those ten days, however, all the resolve and faith of the Israelites somehow vanished because when Jeremiah reported that the Lord said they shouldn't fear the king of Babylon and that if they formed an alliance with Egypt, they'd be destroyed, the people called him a liar (Jeremiah 43:2). They turned to Egypt for protection anyway, and all the prophesied consequences followed.

Ten days. That's all it took for their faithful resolve to collapse into fearful disobedience. Satan would have us believe such a fast reversal could never happen to us, that we are better—our faith stronger—than the Israelites of old. He would have us think ourselves immune to him, that "all is well in Zion" and that it always will be, thus lulling us away into "carnal security" (2 Nephi 28:21).

We are not immune and must strengthen our defenses every moment. Finding Christ in all things helps with this. Now, just as we can't spend every present moment studying the scriptures or attending the temple, we also won't always have time to sit down and write out lists as part of our Christ-finding efforts. However, the more we practice doing so when we do have the time, the more we will train our thoughts to make spiritual connections and find symbols of Christ on their own while we're out and about living our everyday lives.

A PRESENT FOR OTHERS

The present-day benefits of this training don't bless only our lives; training our minds to find Christ in all things also transforms us into better teachers for others. Christ was a master teacher. He could, and often would, stop and use anything around Him as an object lesson for His disciples. He related spiritual truths to things such as fig trees, baking with yeast, and a speck of dust in someone's eye (see Matthew 24:29–33, 13:33, and 7:1–5 respectively). The more we practice this same skill of finding symbols in everything around us, the more we will be able to hear a child's tale of recess mayhem and tie it back into the gospel or transform a friend's dilemma at work into a faith-promoting parable. When we learn to find Christ in all things, we can make any moment a teaching moment, thus more consistently pointing the people in our lives back to Christ.

"And we talk of Christ, we rejoice in Christ, we preach of Christ, we prophesy of Christ, and we write according to our prophecies, that our children may know to what source they may look for a remission of their sins" (2 Nephi 25:26).

A FUTURE HARVEST

Every time we practice finding symbols of Christ in the objects and events of our lives, we are not only blessing ourselves with an immediate fortification of the Spirit, but as Paul admonished, we are "laying up in store for [our]selves a good foundation against the time to come" (1 Timothy 6:19). Every time we practice finding Christ, we are planting a seed for a future harvest as well. When, after continual practice, we arrive at the point that finding symbols of Christ has become a habit, we will have built up a wealth of spiritual parallels and stories that we can draw from for any talks or lessons we may need to give.

The process of seeking Christ through symbolism converts us.

Another future benefit is that as the children in our lives see us practicing this skill and hear us making these connections, they will learn to do it too. We can leave a legacy of Christ-finding for generations to come.

My mission president often reminded us that the most important convert we would ever have was ourselves, and I testify that the Christ-finding process is a conversion process. As we consistently seek Christ in the world around us, something inside us changes.

When asked why He taught in parables, the Lord said it was to keep those with hardened hearts from understanding the truths He taught. But in that same rebuke, He taught the principle that those who "see with their eyes, and hear with their ears, and . . . understand with their heart . . . should be converted" (Matthew 13:15).

In other words, the process of softening our hearts to understand parables and seek Christ through their symbolism converts us. The more we seek Him, the more we'll learn about Him and His nature. The more we learn of Him, the more we'll become like Him.

Moroni taught, "When he shall appear we shall be like him, for we shall see him as he is" (Moroni 7:48). He was speaking of a future literal appearance of the Savior, but I believe it applies symbolically as well. To see Christ "as he is" is to see Him in all things, and when we do that—when we seek Christ in all things—not only will we find Him, but when He appears physically before us one day, whether on this earth or when we leave mortality behind, we will be like Him because the very act of seeking Him in all things will have converted and refined us.

TAKE THE TIME

"And in the morning, rising up a great while before day, he went out, and departed into a solitary place, and there prayed."

MARK 1:35

MUSCLE MEMORY

As a piano player, I've learned the tremendous value of a concept called muscle memory. Our muscles are capable of essentially "memorizing" a particular action and how it feels, so they can perform that movement automatically while our brain focuses on other things.

Let's test it out. I want you to lift your hand in front of you and pretend you are gripping a pencil. Go on. Just lift your hand like you are holding a pencil.

Now, study your fingers. How quickly were you able to accomplish the task? How much thought went into calculating the distance between fingers? How accurate is the spacing between them? Go find a pencil if you want to check. Chances are, your spacing is pretty accurate, and you quickly assumed that position with little to no thought. Why? Muscle memory. You have picked up a pencil and written with it so many times, it is second nature to you now.

The same thing has happened to me as a pianist. At any given moment, I can stretch my pinky and thumb a certain distance apart and know it's the interval of an octave (meaning if I were to place my hand on a keyboard, my fingers would fall on a C and the next highest C). I can do this not only with octaves, but with every interval played by a single hand.

Beyond stationary intervals, I've even been able to close my eyes and accurately jump from one part of the piano to the other, consistently landing on the exact note I want. How? Because I practiced that jump so many times, my muscles memorized the movement.

While the brain isn't technically a muscle, the principle of muscle memory still applies, and it is the end goal of our training in this book. We want finding Christ in our lives to become second nature, an automatic reflex. Such a skill can only be achieved through consistent, dedicated efforts.

THE DANGER OF DISTRACTION

When should we set aside time to practice finding Him? How much time do we need? Those answers will vary according to each person and their circumstances, but I have found that in my life, no matter how busy or relaxed my schedule is, when it comes to working on my goals, saying "I'll try to find some time each day" is never enough.

If I am not specific as to when I will do it, in most cases, it does not get done.

Case in point—piano lessons. Not only do I play the piano, but I teach it as well, as did my mother. Yet despite having one of the best piano teachers I know for a mom, I always took lessons from someone else. And when I started my own studio, I also taught children of other piano teachers.

At first, I didn't understand why it was supposedly so difficult to teach your own children to play. I assumed the problem lay somewhere in the dynamic of never being able to practice without your teacher nearby hearing every note. Growing up, I found it immensely frustrating to have my practicing interrupted by a voice from the next room singing how the melody should have sounded or asking if I had double-checked the tempo markings.

But while that could be a contributing factor, the real reason for the difficulty of teaching your own children didn't become apparent to me until I had children of my own and vowed that I would teach them myself.

Turns out, the biggest issue in teaching my own children is having the actual lessons. A key benefit to teaching your own kids is flexibility. If life happens and you need to push the lesson back, you can push it back. The problem with that flexibility, however, is that my plan to teach the kids "sometime on Friday afternoons," often results in them coming home from school, unwinding with a snack, and getting distracted with toys. Meanwhile, I get distracted with chores, writing, or catching up on social media.

Before I know it, it's time for dinner. Then bedtime. I always say, "We'll make up the lesson tomorrow," but tomorrow becomes next week, which then becomes the week after that. When they were younger, I would look over their practice notebooks at the end of the year and find that we averaged one lesson every two or three weeks at best. And as they've grown older and our lives have gathered even more distractions, it is now often months between lessons.

I always have the best of intentions and often narrow down a general time to try and have the lessons. Yet without actually scheduling a time and committing to not scheduling other things on top of it, my intentions often fail to produce the desired results.

I've found this to be the case for every righteous goal I set. The adversary is cunning. He has spent a lot of time studying us and learning our weaknesses, which is why he knows that sometimes he can outright tempt us with sin, and we'll take the bait.

In addition to our weaknesses, however, Satan also knows our strengths. He knows that in some cases, blatant temptation is ineffective, which is why he has many weapons in his arsenal.

One weapon Satan uses against me all the time is distraction. I've learned that Satan doesn't need us to do bad things, he simply needs us to be so busy doing good things that we neglect doing the best things. He might not be able to keep us from being worthy to hold a temple recommend, but if he can keep us too busy to ever go to the temple, is it not a victory for him just the same?

Success doesn't come simply by knowing what we want. We have to decide which of our wants and desires take priority over the others and not let anything get in the way of those priorities.

Consider the parable of the talents (Matthew 25:14–30). Prior to taking a trip, a lord entrusted three servants with different amounts of talents (money). The servants who received two and five talents invested them, while the servant who received only one talent buried his. When the lord returned, he praised the first two servants for doubling his money and condemned the last servant for burying the talent and wasting the investment opportunity.

But what if the servant who received one talent hadn't buried it? Suppose he'd had every intention of doing what the other servants had done, maybe he'd even kept the talent in his pocket to always have on hand, but he got so sidetracked by other priorities that he forgot to go to the financial markets and invest it. Would the reckoning with his lord have gone any different?

I doubt it. Not if he consistently gave his "more earnest heed" to other things in his life, showing his lord what his priorities really were (Hebrews 2:1).

On the other hand, if the servant had earnestly kept trying to get to the market, but obstacle after obstacle beyond his control prevented him from being able to follow through with this desire, I'm sure the lord would've had compassion. After all, the Lord "is a discerner of the thoughts and intents of the heart" (D&C 33:1). The takeaway here is that success doesn't come simply by knowing what we want. We have to decide which of our wants and desires take priority over the others and not let anything get in the way of those priorities.

We must "attend upon the Lord without distraction" (1 Corinthians 7:35).

TIMES AND TRIGGERS

Now that we've discussed the importance of avoiding distractions by scheduling and dedicating a specific time to practicing this Christ-finding process, let's look at a few examples of what those specific times could look like.

For some, adding a few extra minutes of meditation time in their morning scripture study is a great opportunity because the scriptures are full of symbols and stories that make excellent practice. For others, reflecting over the day's events during evening prayer and picking one event to use as practice might be a more helpful goal. Even consistently practicing once a week during a Sabbath day journaling session would yield a spiritual form of muscle memory over time.

If you wish to make it a family effort, you could incorporate practice time into family home evening, challenging each member to share something that happened to them that week and working together as a family to find symbols of Christ in it. Or during family dinners, you could try the game my seminary students and I played—one person picks any object, and another person has to relate it to the Savior.

When it comes to progress, direction is *always* more important than speed.

If your schedule is already so full that another item simply won't fit, don't despair. While training our minds to find Christ in all things takes practice, and practice is ideally done on a consistent basis, it's important to acknowledge our limitations. True, my kids would progress much faster at the piano if I gave them consistent weekly lessons or paid someone else to do it, but the sporadic lessons they have are still better than nothing. They've still progressed, albeit slowly.

When it comes to progress, direction is *always* more important than speed.

If you find yourself in a position where you can't set aside a specific time of day to consistently practice finding symbols of Christ, another possibility is to set aside a certain event that can function as a trigger to remind you to practice. Your trigger could be something as simple as a red traffic light; anytime you stop at one, that's your cue to pick one object in your line of sight and relate it back to Christ.

Other possible triggers could be frustration, stress, sadness, or anger. Whenever something is hard or you're in a bad mood, let that be your mental signal to stop and ask "What is frustrating me, and what can it teach me about Christ?"

I've found two advantages to using negative emotions as triggers. First, as a flawed mortal for whom stressing comes as naturally as breathing, I experience negative emotions frequently, so using them as a trigger provides me with *a lot* of repetition to develop my spiritual muscle memory. Another advantage is that by turning my thoughts to Christ, I invite the Spirit to be with me, and my mood invariably improves.

Joy or gratitude can also be used as triggers. Since they are fruits of the Spirit, they make it easier to find comparisons between everyday items and our Lord and His gospel because the Spirit is already present, priming our minds to think of eternal things.

Another possible trigger you could use is a bad habit you wish to break. If all we do is sweep our bad habits out, we may find that they come back stronger than before (Luke 11:24–26). But if we replace them with good habits, there won't be room for them to re-enter our lives. What could be a better replacement than the habit of finding Christ in all things?

If you want to give up swearing or stop impure or judgmental thoughts, anytime you feel the urge to say or think those things, let it be an alarm to your mind that says it's time to implement your training. Pick the item nearest to you, or the last thing you did, and follow the process in this book to tie it back to Christ.

TIPS AND A PROMISE

Whether your plan involves consistent triggers or consistent scheduled times, using reminders such as alarms on your phone or sticky notes on your bathroom mirror can increase your odds of success.

Having an accountability partner is also highly beneficial. If you work on this training with a spouse, with a friend, or together as a family, your accountability partners are built in, but I know from personal experience that Heavenly Father is more than happy to be an accountability partner as well. Reporting to Him at the end of each day is a great motivator. Recording your efforts in a journal or progress chart can help keep you accountable as well. I've even started a Facebook group called "Finding Christ in Your Daily Life" where we can gather as a community to hold each other accountable.

When it comes to training your mind to see Christ in all things, it doesn't matter whether you choose a specific trigger or a certain hour of the day to practice. What matters most is that you make a plan and do your best to stick to it. The usefulness of training your brain to find Christ in all things is directly related to your willingness to actually take the time to search for Him.

The adversary will try and distract you. He will try to keep you too busy to look for Christ. He will tell you that you don't have time to add anything else to your schedule or the mental energy to think about one more thing. But I promise that if you make a specific plan to seek Christ and do your best to stick to that plan, your remaining time and energy will be sufficient to accomplish every necessary thing.

"But seek ye first the kingdom of God, and his righteousness; and all these things shall be added unto you" (Matthew 6:33).

WRITE AND RECORD

"And the Lord answered me and said, Write the vision, and make it plain upon tables, that he may run that readeth it."

HABAKKUK 2:2

FROM THE FINGERNAILS OF BABES

As a mother of young children, few words were more frightening to me than *permanent marker*. When my three oldest boys were young, I worked hard to keep every permanent marker or ink pen out of their reach, and I felt fairly confident that my efforts had paid off and that I had successfully childproofed my home from the dangers of permanent writing implements.

Poor, naive me.

One particular day, when my children were six, four, and two, my oldest came and informed me that my four-year-old was "scratching the couch." I followed him to the living room and discovered my son Evan sitting on the couch, scratching purposefully at the brown leather armrest. When I asked what he was doing, he proudly announced he was writing his name, a skill he had recently learned in preschool. He sat back so I could admire his handiwork, and to my dismay, behind his chubby, proudly beaming face was the letter *E*—carved into the brown leather not once, but twice, by his stubby little fingers.

In the months that followed, nothing I did made those finger-drawn *E*'s go away. They were still there when we eventually sold the couch at a garage sale.

I learned a few very important lessons from this experience. First, no matter how diligently you hide the permanent markers, your kids will still find a way to leave their permanent mark on things.

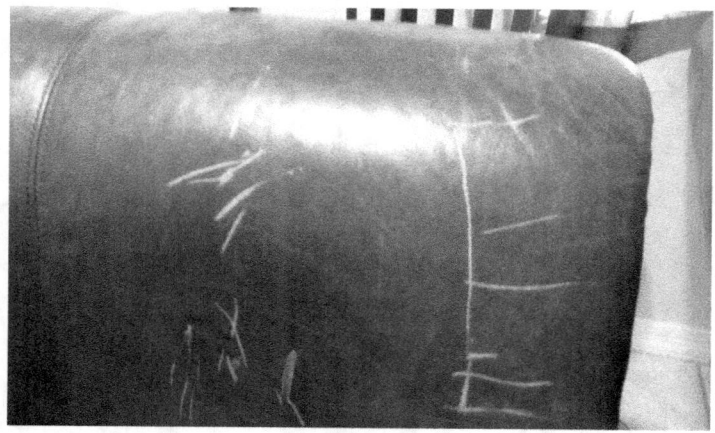

Second, as much as it pained me to see what Evan had done to our couch, I realized my son had taught me an important principle of learning. Thinking about how to spell his name wasn't nearly as helpful as actually writing it down. There is a powerful facet of our learning that comes when we actually put pen to paper (or nail to leather).

TO WRITE OR NOT TO WRITE

As we walk through the steps of this process together, I will often mention making lists and writing things down. I understand that it isn't feasible to record your thought process every time you implement this training, especially if you're practicing while driving or when triggered by certain emotions. Written lists may be the ideal, but it's absolutely still possible to make mental lists and find symbols of Christ. Before I started writing this book, I made all my connections mentally without writing them down.

However, in trying to deconstruct my process into steps others could follow, I challenged myself to record each step—to write out questions about the subject and answer them, list all the possible symbols found in those answers, and fill out a chart with details about each one. To make sure my process could truly work at all times and with all things, I picked one of the most seemingly banal and inconsequential verses in scripture to practice on: "And my father dwelt in a tent" (1 Nephi 2:15).

The exact details of what I wrote and learned about that verse are discussed in chapter 10, but when I finished writing everything down and stared at my lists, I had chills. I sat on my bed, stunned. The Spirit enlightened me in such a way that I couldn't believe I had previously dismissed that verse as some unimportant commentary on nomadic dwellings.

I firmly believe the revelation I received that day would not have happened if I had only been thinking about everything. It was the written details of the lists I made and seeing all the elements spelled out next to each other that enabled my mind to grasp the big picture the Spirit was trying to teach me.

Do you have to write and record the steps of this process in order to benefit from it? No. If Christ can work a miracle with a few loaves and fishes, He can certainly make something happen with just your memory and the few minutes you're driving in the car trying to think of Him.

But I testify that writing and recording can increase the quality and consistency of revelation. It does for me, every time.

TWO METHODS ARE BETTER THAN ONE

The act of writing has been scientifically proven to result in a greater capacity to learn and recall information. (Studies have even shown that handwriting the information, as opposed to typing, further increases understanding and retention.[1])

The science behind this idea stems from two facts:

---

1. Pam A. Mueller and Daniel M. Oppenheimer, "The Pen Is Mightier Than the Keyboard: Advantages of Longhand Over Laptop Note Taking," *Psychological Science*, vol. 25, no. 6 (2014), 1159–68.

First, the human brain is divided into different sections, each with its own unique functions. The portion of your brain responsible for vision (occipital lobe) is different than the part responsible for hearing (temporal lobe), which is also different than the part responsible for touch (parietal lobe). Balance and coordination, speech production, and breathing are each governed by their own unique brain regions as well.

Writing something increases your ability to learn and recall it.

Second, the more areas of your brain you use when learning a specific concept, the more likely you are to truly learn and retain that concept. Neurologist Dr. Judy Willis wrote, "The more regions of the brain that store data about a subject, the more interconnection there is. This redundancy means students will have more opportunities to pull up all of those related bits of data from their multiple storage areas in response to a single cue. This cross-referencing of data means we have learned, rather than just memorized."[2]

So if you use your cognitive skills to think about an idea, your motor skills to write it down, and your visual recognition to read the words you just put on paper, you've used not one but three different areas of your brain. Hence, writing leads to a greater ability to learn and recall.

2. Judy Willis, "Review of Research: Brain-Based Teaching Strategies for Improving Students' Memory, Learning, and Test-Taking Success," *Childhood Education*, vol. 83, no. 5 (2007), 310–315.

If you aren't in a position to write things down, you can still apply the concept of enlisting multiple regions of your brain to deepen your learning by thinking about your ideas, speaking the thoughts aloud, and hearing your own words.

REVELATION BEGINS WITH PRAYER

The idea that engaging multiple senses promotes better learning isn't a recent discovery; it's an eternal principle of how we were designed to acquire knowledge. When Oliver Cowdery wanted to learn the art of translation, God told him that the Holy Ghost would speak to his mind *and* his heart, using not one method but two, thus providing a deeper level of understanding and assurance (D&C 8:2).

But while God told Oliver he could expect revelation to come to his mind and his heart, He didn't promise to simply give Oliver the answers. That knowledge was conditional upon Oliver asking in faith (D&C 8:1).

Asking in faith has been a prerequisite to revelation all throughout the scriptures. After Lehi had his vision of the tree of life, he shared it with his family. The vision was highly symbolic, and his sons struggled to understand its meaning. While their confusion was the same, their approaches to trying to understand the symbolism were very different.

Nephi "sat pondering in [his] heart," all the while "believing that the Lord was able to make [the meaning of his father's vision] known unto [him]" (1 Nephi 11:1). His desire, faith, and willingness to sit and ponder resulted in him receiving his own amazing vision that explained his father's (1 Nephi 11–14).

Nephi's older brothers, Laman and Lemuel, had the same desire to know. But they didn't have faith, and they didn't put in any effort. When Nephi found them arguing and complaining about not understanding their father's vision, he asked them, "Have ye inquired of the Lord?" (1 Nephi 15:8). They replied, "We have not" (1 Nephi 15:9).

You can't expect an answer to a question you haven't asked.

Like Nephi, let us be willing to request revelation in faith by beginning our study with a prayer. As we do, the Lord will provide answers. He will still expect us to study things out in our minds (D&C 9:7–9), but we should never be fooled into pridefully thinking that our insights come solely because of our own mental studies. Even though the process detailed in this book is meant to train our brains to make spiritual connections, when the connections come, they will not be our doing. They will be revelation. A gift freely given if we ask for it and work for it.

I've found that when I am prepared to receive revelation, I receive it more frequently. Part of that preparation is praying for it, and another is having the means and intent to record, keep, and treasure it. I once had an institute professor tell me that having a pen out during class was like putting up an antenna to receive revelation. I like to think of my pen and paper as forming a velvet-lined box. By getting them ready, I show the Spirit that I'm ready to receive the treasures of knowledge He will give, instead of letting those truths get misplaced and ignored in the muddiness of my mortal mind.

Our memories are paper chains at best, distorting and dissolving in the waters of time. They cannot reliably tether us to our spiritual anchors.

ANCHORS AND CHAINS

While implementing the steps of this Christ-finding process, some of the revelations I've received have come as small, simple thoughts—little insights and connections that reminded me of Christ for a wonderful moment and then were gone. Other revelations, however, have been game changers—eye-opening, soul-stirring witnesses that continue to serve as spiritual anchors in my life.

But what good is an anchor without a chain to keep us connected to it?

This is where having a written record is such a blessing. Some people rely solely on their memories to tether them to their anchoring spiritual experiences. But have you ever gone back and watched a movie you loved as a child, only to realize as an adult that it was nothing like you remembered? Have you ever looked at an old photo and not been able to recall the name of a friend or classmate you once knew so well? Our memories are paper chains at best, distorting and dissolving in the waters of time. They cannot reliably tether us to our spiritual anchors. Writing down the inspiration and revelations we receive (and reading and reviewing those records) connects us to our revelatory experiences with reliable chains that time cannot so easily erode.

SELECT THE SUBJECT

"Whether to the north or to the south, to the east or to the west, it mattereth not, for ye cannot go amiss."

DOCTRINE AND COVENANTS 80:3

WHERE TO LOOK

Once we've taken the time and are ready to write and record (if possible), it's time to select the subject for our Christ-finding exercise.

As previously mentioned, you can look anywhere for your inspiration. There really is no right or wrong way to choose your subject. Pick the most memorable thing that happened to you last week. Your favorite scripture story or verse. The first thing you see when you wake up.

The whole premise of this exercise is that anything can be a type and shadow of Christ, so any subject will work. The only mistake you can make is spending so much time brainstorming the "right" subject that you fail to select any subject at all.

TYPES OF SUBJECTS

To illustrate the range of subjects available for our Christ-finding practice, I've created three subject categories of varying complexity. I'll use examples from each of these categories over the next few chapters to show how the process will apply to each type of subject.

1. THE SINGLE OBJECT

The only requirement for this type of subject is that it must be a noun—a person, place, or thing. Single objects can be things like a pet shop, a crossing guard, or a hand-crank flashlight.

2. THE SIMPLE SITUATION

A simple situation subject usually involves one or two nouns and a verb. It isn't a complete story; there isn't necessarily a beginning, middle, and end, nor any kind of conflict. It's just a situation, such as getting a tire alignment, having to match up socks on laundry day, or kids making a mess with toothpaste. It doesn't have to be anything riveting. Mundane situations work just as well as extraordinary ones.

3. THE COMPLETE STORY

The last type of subject you might consider selecting is a complete story. This is something with a beginning, a middle, and an end, and there's usually some degree of conflict. Examples include my lasagna fiasco at the beginning of this book or a scripture story such as when David slew Goliath.

DON'T DISMISS THE SIMPLE

Nothing is too simple or basic to count as a subject. There are questions we can ask about single objects or simple situations to help flesh them out, giving us plenty of material to work with during our Christ-finding process. As you'll see in future examples, there is meat to be had on even the boniest of subjects, so beware dismissing any subject due to its initial simplicity.

The Israelites of old provide a great cautionary tale about the risks associated with overlooking simple things. When they were afflicted by fiery flying serpents, God commanded Moses to form a serpent and lift it up on a pole, and anyone who looked on the brass serpent Moses had made would live (Numbers 21:5–9). Nephi recounted this story to his brothers, with some insightful commentary as well:

> And he did straiten them in the wilderness with his rod; for they hardened their hearts, even as ye have; and the Lord straitened them because of their iniquity. He sent fiery flying serpents among them; and after they were bitten he prepared a way that they might be healed; *and the labor which they had to perform was to look; and because of the*

simpleness of the way, or the easiness of it, there were many
who perished. (1 Nephi 17:41, emphasis added)

Many of the afflicted didn't look, and they died as a result. They missed out on a major blessing because looking at the brass serpent seemed too simple. Likewise, we can miss out on major insights and revelations if we reject simple situations or single objects out of fear that they're too basic.

Remember that the Savior, the master teacher, didn't teach His disciples using only complete stories like that of the Good Samaritan. He also used single objects, like a mustard seed or yeast, to teach important principles. Single objects and simple situations carry the additional benefit of being more abundant in everyday life, thus providing more examples with which to practice finding Christ.

WHAT TO WRITE: SINGLE OBJECTS

Compared to complete stories and even simple situations, single objects can seem woefully sparse in detail. Fleshing them out so you have enough material to work with can be done by asking a few questions about your object. You can ask any questions you feel would be helpful, but here are a few I like to use:

- *Who uses the object?*
- *When or where would they use this object?*
- *What is it used for?*
- *How is it used?*
- *What materials or components is the object made of?*

Let's use a hand-crank flashlight as our single object example. Everyone might answer these questions differently, but my fleshed-out notes look like this.

What is the object?	Hand-crank flashlight
Who uses the object?	Any human who wants light
When or where would they use this object?	When it's dark and they don't want to (or can't) rely on electricity or batteries for light
What is it used for?	To create a small amount of light
How is it used?	The crank is turned repeatedly to create kinetic energy to power the bulb; the light dims quickly and must be constantly re-cranked to keep the power going
What materials or components is the object made of?	LED bulb, reflectors, power button, hand crank, gears, wires, battery, generator

WHAT TO WRITE: SIMPLE SITUATIONS

Simple situations have more details built into them than single objects, but finding Christ in simple situations is easier if we flesh them out with some additional questions as well. Here are some questions I often ask to guide me in fleshing out and better understanding a simple situation.

- *Is this situation normal? If not, what does normal look like?*
- *What events lead up to this situation?*
- *What events follow this situation?*
- *Who or what does this situation affect?*
- *Is this situation (and/or its effects) desirable? If so, how is it brought about? If not desirable, how can it be avoided? In either case, are there obstacles that must be overcome?*
- *How often does this situation occur?*
- *What objects would be used to get into or out of this situation?*

For our simple situation example, let's use kids making a mess with toothpaste. If you don't have children or can't picture what such a dental crime scene might look like, allow me to take you back to when I was a mother of three young boys and show you what their bathroom looked like on a particular day.

 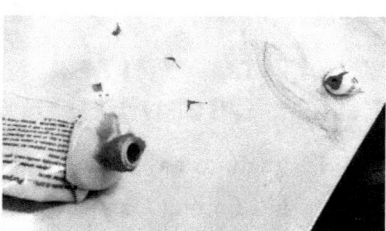

Photo 1. Photo 2.

With the photos being printed in black and white, you can't appreciate the vibrant shade of "sparkle fun" blue paste gunking up the mouth of each toothpaste tube (unless of course, you've seen such oral hygiene carnage in your own home). But for the record, if you've ever wondered what a frozen waterfall looks like during a Minnesota winter, my children recreated it for you in Photo 1.

I wish I could say that Photo 2 featured the same pair of tubes photographed on a different day, but no. Those are two *different* toothpaste tubes, on a different section of the bathroom counter, photographed at the same time as those in Photo 1. Which means on that day we had not one, not two, but *four* tubes of messy toothpaste strewn around. And I only had three kids at the time.

Not pictured are the lids that once belonged to these four tubes. Every single one had vanished, and their locations were a baffling mystery (much like the company's use of "sparkle fun" as a flavor description). Also not pictured, though equally baffling, are the smears of blue toothpaste I would often find on the outside of the bathtub. Once, I even found toothpaste smears behind the toilet. For the sake of my sanity, I try not to imagine how they got there.

Now that we're all on the same page as to what the situation "kids make a mess with toothpaste" looks like (in my home, at least), here's what my fleshed-out notes for this situation would be.

What is the situation?	Kids make a mess with toothpaste
Is this situation normal? If not, what does normal look like?	For kids, it's normal; for adults, less mess is normal
What events lead up to this situation?	Messy tube mouth = squeezing out more than needed and not wiping off excess, making it hard to screw on lid; unused lids get lost
	Messy counter/tub = dropping toothbrush while goofing off, wandering around instead of standing in front of the sink
	Multiple tubes = not squeezing from bottom, feeling like the tube has run out when it hasn't, easier to open a new tube than to put in the work of cleaning off old one and pushing out what's left
What events follow this situation?	Lots of scrubbing, missing more entertaining things because they have to clean, pain from stepping on random lids
	Longer brushing sessions as parent demonstrates yet again how squeezing from the bottom can result in more toothpaste magically appearing from what seemed like an empty tube

Who or what does this situation affect?	The whole family
	Kids get chided, lose story time, have extra work to do
	Parents are frustrated because there's always a mess and it wastes money
Is this situation (and/or its effects) desirable? If so, how is it brought about? If not desirable, how can it be avoided? In either case, are there obstacles that must be overcome?	Mess is not desirable, could be avoided if kids took time to push from the bottom, wipe off excess, and put the lid back on each time; also if they stood still while brushing
	Mom or Dad could load the toothbrushes for them and supervise each brushing session
	Effects of brushing, despite the mess, are desirable (clean breath and healthy teeth)
	Kids' obstacles = underdeveloped hand-eye coordination and lack of patience when they're eager to brush quickly and move on to something more enjoyable
	Parents' obstacles = fatigue and lack of desire to supervise each session
How often does this situation occur?	Typically 1–2 times per day
What objects would be used to get into or out of this situation?	To make mess: their hands, toothbrushes, tubes, toothpaste in the tubes, lids, counter, tub, sink
	To fix mess: water, rags, time, patience, experience, coordination

WHAT TO WRITE: COMPLETE STORIES

If you select a complete story as your subject, begin by writing down the story with as many details as you can. You can write in a series of paragraphs, a list of bullet points, or anything else that makes sense to you. The key is to include as many details as you can now, so you'll have more material to work with later.

> **The more details you include now, the more material you'll have to work with later.**

If you want to mine your story for more details, you could consider what happened just before the story started or if there were any events going on behind the scenes while the story unfolded that made the story possible.

In addition to using this Christ-finding process with events in my life, I enjoy applying it to the scriptures as well. Using this process has helped me uncover additional insights and deeper meaning in scripture stories I assumed I already understood. Since we already have some examples from real life (a handcrank flashlight and kids making a mess with toothpaste), let's take a look at a scripture for our complete story example. We'll use the story of David and Goliath, as found in 1 Samuel 17.

Now, I could simply use the chapter directly from the scriptures, whether printing out the verses verbatim to make notes on or using my digital scriptures to highlight and notate as needed. However, I want to illustrate how to write out a complete story, whether from your life or the scriptures, so here's an example using bullet points:

DAVID AND GOLIATH

- The Philistines and the Israelites (led by King Saul) had come together to battle.
- The Philistines sent out a champion named Goliath, who was over six cubits tall and had heavy brass armor, a massive spear and shield, and a shield bearer.
- Goliath challenged the Israelites to send their own champion for a winner-takes-all duel. Saul and the Israelites were afraid to send anyone.
- David was Jesse's youngest son. His three oldest brothers were away in the Israelite army. As shepherd for his dad's sheep, he fought off a bear and a lion.
- David's dad sent him to take food (corn, loaves, and ten cheeses) to his brothers and their leaders to see how they were doing. David woke early, made sure someone else was caring for the sheep, and headed to the battle.
- David heard Goliath defy Israel and tried to get someone to stand up to him. When no one would, David went to King Saul and offered to battle Goliath himself.

Stress hinders the Spirit, so do your best, then let it rest. It will be enough.

- Saul said David was too young and inexperienced. David told him about defeating the bear and lion. His faith was so strong, Saul agreed to let him go.

- Saul offered David his own armor and sword. David declined. Now wasn't the time to experiment with new things. Instead, he took his staff and shepherd's sling, and five stones from a nearby brook.

- David approached Goliath. Goliath vowed to feed his dead body to the birds. David replied that the birds would feast on Goliath and the whole Philistine army, then said, "The Lord saveth not with sword and spear: for the battle is the Lord's, and he will give you into our hands" (verse 47).

- Goliath came toward David. David ran to meet him, pulled a stone from his bag, slung it, and hit Goliath on the forehead. Goliath fell, dead.

You don't have to write down every single detail of your complete story; I didn't list the individual pieces of Goliath's armor, the keeper of the carriage, or any of the details about David beheading Goliath or the battle that followed his death. It's true that the more you write up front, the more potential insights you'll have later in the process, but don't let yourself feel overwhelmed or stressed about missing some part of the story. Stress is a hindrance to feeling the Spirit, and the Spirit is a vital part of this process. So do your best, then let it rest. It will be enough.

FINAL CAUTIONS AND ENCOURAGEMENT

As you write down as much as you can for whatever subject you've selected, don't worry about making connections to Christ yet. If inspiration strikes, definitely seize the opportunity and skip right ahead to chapter eight. But if, as you're writing, you don't know what anything could symbolize, that's okay. It will come.

Also, don't be afraid to do a little research. I wasn't entirely sure what was on the inside of a hand-crank flashlight when I started writing this chapter. After a quick Internet search, I found out it involved gears, generators, and batteries. Do I fully understand the mechanics and science behind hand-crank flashlights now? No. But I understand enough to write down the components, and if later in the process I become inspired to make parallels to those components, I can do more research. At this stage, we are mainly focused on gathering all our materials. We may not wind up using every element we've fleshed out here, but gathering it all now gives us more to potentially work with later.

PICK THE PLAYERS

"His eye seeth every precious thing."

JOB 28:10

DEFINING PLAYERS

Imagine you're a sports coach, trying to create a winning team. Before you choose who should be the team captain or who to put in as a starting player, you need to know exactly who is on your team roster. You need to know who your players are.

In the Christ-finding process, we'll do essentially the same thing. First we'll put together a roster of potential symbols (pick the players). Next we'll take some time to get to know each player (dig for details), and finally we'll start assigning players to their positions (match to the Master).

In our case, a player is any noun (person, place, or thing) involved in your subject. So to pick all your players, you'll look at what you wrote about your subject, including any questions and answers you used to expand it, then simply circle or highlight any noun you see and make a separate list of just those nouns.

> A player is any noun (person, place, or thing) involved in your subject.

EXAMPLES OF PLAYERS: HAND-CRANK FLASHLIGHT

When you're working with a single object, it may seem like there is only a single player, but if we go back to those questions from the last chapter, we'll find many more nouns involved with a hand-crank flashlight. Look at all the players (nouns) I've bolded from the original chart:

What is the object?	**Hand-crank flashlight**
Who uses the object?	Any **human** who wants light
When or where would they use this object?	When **it's dark** and they don't want to (or can't) rely on electricity or batteries for light
What is it used for?	To create a small amount of **light**
How is it used?	**The crank is turned** repeatedly to create **kinetic energy** to power the **bulb**; the light dims quickly and must **be constantly re-cranked** to keep the power going
What materials or components is the object made of?	LED bulb, **reflectors**, **power button**, hand crank, **gears**, **wires**, **battery**, **generator**

If a player repeats, I only bold it once. I also didn't bold all the players (such as electricity and batteries in the third row)—if you miss some players, it'll be fine. The goal of this process isn't "perfection." We're simply gathering enough potential symbols to make our job of finding Christ easier when the time comes.

Some players are sneaky. Notice the phrase *it's dark*. The word *it* is technically a pronoun, and *dark* is technically an adjective. But if we combine both words into a single idea, we get the noun *darkness* which is the player we would write.

"The act of [verb]ing" counts as a noun.

You can also transform key verbs into nouns in order to add them to your roster of players. Simply change the verb's ending to -ing and preface it with "the act of."

"Is turned" (verb) becomes "the act of turning" (noun).

"Be re-cranked" (verb) becomes "the act of re-cranking" (noun).

If a better phrasing comes to mind than how you originally wrote it, go ahead and alter it. For example, "the act of turning (the crank)" might be better as "the act of cranking."

If English 101 isn't your thing and all this talk of nouns and verbs has you feeling like you're in over your head, don't worry. Throw the grammar book out and think in terms of "potential symbols." All we're doing when we pick the players is putting together a list of potential symbols to further consider.

Based on what I bolded earlier in our chart, my list of players for a hand-crank flashlight would look like this:

PLAYERS INVOLVED WITH HAND-CRANK FLASHLIGHT

Hand-crank flashlight

Human

Darkness

Light

Crank

The act of cranking

Kinetic energy

Bulb

The act of re-cranking

Reflectors

Power button

Gears

Wires

Battery

Generator

EXAMPLES OF PLAYERS: KIDS MAKING A MESS WITH TOOTHPASTE

For our example of kids making a mess with toothpaste, if we review the questions we answered in the last chapter about this subject, then circle, highlight, or bold any nouns (including verbs converted to nouns), our list of players might look like this.

PLAYERS INVOLVED IN KIDS MAKING A MESS WITH TOOTHPASTE

Kids

Adults

Bathroom

Mess

Toothpaste

Toothpaste tube

Lid to the toothpaste tube

The act of squeezing out too much

The act of squeezing from the bottom

The act of believing there's no toothpaste left

The act of wandering around or goofing off

Extra tubes of toothpaste

Cleaning supplies

Pain

Teeth

Hand-eye coordination

Patience

Experience

EXAMPLES OF PLAYERS: DAVID AND GOLIATH

As for our complete story, if I were to list out the players from my notes about the story of David and Goliath, my list might look like this:

PLAYERS INVOLVED IN THE DAVID AND GOLIATH STORY
Philistine army
Israelite army
Standoff
Goliath
Goliath's armor
Goliath's challenge
David
Sheep
Bear and lion
Jesse
Corn and loaves
Ten cheeses
Keeper of sheep
King Saul
Saul's armor
David's staff
David's sling
Brook
Stones
The act of running to meet Goliath
The act of slinging a stone

At this point, you might be thinking these lists are overkill. After all, the story of David and Goliath is clearly about God helping us overcome our trials no matter how big those trials are. Does it really make a difference whether we list the ten cheeses or the keeper of the sheep?

It could. Let me explain why.

ONE PERSON'S TRASH

My mother is one of the most creative people I know. When I was growing up, she went through different artistic phases. Stamping and embossing were a big thing for a while in our home. Later, it was dried flowers and floral arranging. When I was a young newlywed, she started making what she called "upcycled apothecary jars" with her sisters. These jars were elegant glass containers with oil-rubbed bronze bases and lids.

As stunning as they looked, the real shocker was what they were made of—fishbowls and ashtrays, shower curtain hooks and teacups, plastic beads and wooden spools. The types of things my mother would find at thrift stores and manage to turn into the perfect base or lid astounded me.

Now, most of those materials were not acquired with a specific jar in mind. Our house overflowed with boxes of random, seemingly

Photo credit Jennie Blaser

The potential
for great
revelation
exists in even
the smallest or
most mundane
of things.

useless things. However, those odds and ends were there for her whenever she needed them. Sometimes while constructing a lid, she mixed and matched dozens of different things before finding the perfect fit. By keeping an open mind, she could transform something as trivial and random as a pair of dice or a seashell into part of a uniquely beautiful jar.

ENOUGH IS ENOUGH

Collecting all the seemingly insignificant players upfront can help you build something beautiful later on. Once you make connections, those little elements of your story can be transformed to reveal additional messages and insights that would have remained lost if you hadn't taken the time to ponder and list the more obscure players in your subject. The potential for great revelation exists in even the smallest or most mundane of things. As the prophet Alma said, 'Now ye may suppose that this is foolishness in me; but behold I say unto you, that by small and simple things are great things brought to pass; and small means in many instances doth confound the wise" (Alma 37:6).

As you list your players, however, please don't get overwhelmed trying to write every single possible noun before you continue. Yes, including seemingly insignificant players will give you more material to work with and yield better results than just listing a couple key players, but not if it becomes a distraction that keeps you from moving on to the step of the process that actually yields the results.

How do you know when you have enough players listed? When the Spirit tells you it's enough, when you start to feel overwhelmed and risk losing the Spirit, or even when you simply want to move on. In any of these cases, stop listing players and move on to the next step with faith that the Spirit will help you make wonderful connections with what you've listed so far.

DIG FOR DETAILS

"Let no man count them as small things; for there is much which lieth in futurity . . . which depends upon these things."

DOCTRINE AND COVENANTS 123:15

LET IT SNOW

Growing up in the Sonoran Desert of Arizona, I never had a lot of experience with snow. I can count on my hands the number of times I actually saw the magical white stuff as a child. The first memory I have of it is when I was about six years old. We went to visit my grandparents for Christmas and had just pulled into their snow-lined driveway in Bountiful, Utah, after the twelve-hour drive up from Arizona I was so tired of being in that van and so excited to play in the snow that I jumped out of the car straight into the white embankment.

To the shock and surprise of my naive desert mind, my sneakers, socks, and jeans became instantly soaked. I'd figured it would be cold, but it had never crossed my mind that it would also be wet. That's how little firsthand knowledge of snow I had.

In my early thirties, we moved to Utah for my husband's graduate program. It was my first time living somewhere with snow. There were plenty of storms that first fall and winter. I learned how snow turned muddy and slushy after the plows came through and boots trampled all over it and how it melted and changed from soft, fluffy drifts to hard-packed ice. By January, I felt confident I finally understood all there was to know about snow—what it was, what caused it, and that it was both cold *and* wet.

During a snowfall at the end of January, however, something happened that forever changed the way I looked at snow.

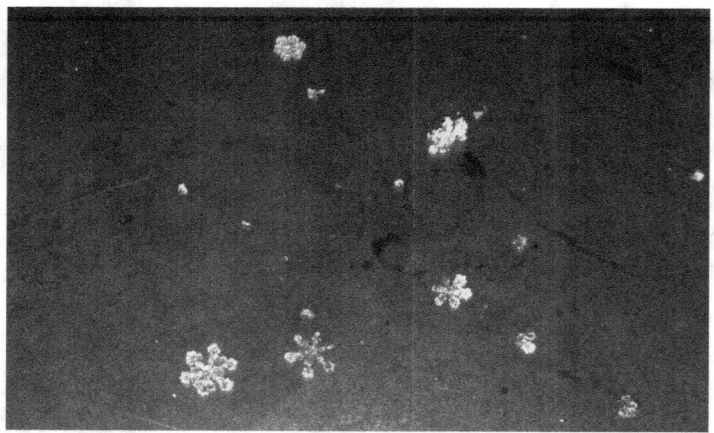

I was carrying groceries into the house, and as I walked around the side of my car, one of the flecks of snow on my sideview mirror seemed odd. It wasn't a round spot like all the others. I stopped to look a little closer and was gobsmacked.

There in the freezing air of my open garage, against the black background of my sideview mirror, I could see all six sides of the individual snowflake. I could see delicate crystallized patterns. And I could see it all with my naked eye!

I had seen pictures of snowflakes before. I had heard the adage that no two snowflakes are ever alike. I had cut snowflake designs out of paper. And yet, in my mind, those were abstract images of snow or perhaps something viewable only at a molecular level under a microscope.

Any time I had seen snow fall before, it had always been tiny flecks or small clumps of white, no more uniquely distinguishable than one drop of rain from another. It had never dawned on me until that day that the flakes falling from the sky were actually individual, fragile, beautiful masterpieces. I spent the next thirty minutes standing in my driveway, catching flakes on my black coat and studying them while my groceries sat in the trunk.

I've learned a lot about snow since that first wet-leg experience in my grandparents' driveway, but the most important thing I've learned is this: no matter how well you think you know something or someone, there are always details you have yet to notice.

No matter
how well you
think you
know some-
thing, there are
always details
you have yet
to notice.

HOW TO DIG FOR DETAILS

Digging for details means listing the characteristics and functions of each player. There's no right or wrong here. Any thought that comes to your mind that describes the player in any way counts as a detail.

Now, there's a reason this step is named *dig* for details, and it's not only because I love alliteration. If you want to make connections and find symbols you haven't thought of before, you need to think about each player in ways you haven't before. You need to ponder each player in-depth.

It can be tempting to write the first adjective that comes to mind for each player and move on, but see what happens when you spend a little more time. List multiple details. Some details will seem obvious, but others won't come until you get the obvious ones out of the way and keep digging.

BE THOU HUMBLE

The key to digging deep is being humble. We must assume we don't know all there is to know, no matter how familiar we are with a subject. If I had assumed I *didn't* really know what snow looked like up close and had taken the time to study snowflakes when the first snow fell in October, I would have discovered the beautiful details of individual snowflakes at the beginning of the season. I could have enjoyed that discovery every time it snowed in November and December as well. As it was, I was lucky that day in January that the isolated white shape on my black mirror caught my eye. If it hadn't, I might have gone on missing the joy of those tiny marvels.

In Doctrine and Covenants 5:24, the Lord made a promise to Martin Harris. He said, "Behold, I say unto him, he exalts himself and does not humble himself sufficiently before me; but if he will bow down before me, and humble himself in mighty prayer and faith, in the sincerity of his heart, then will I grant unto him a view of the things which he desires to see."

I believe that promise is extended to each of us as well. If we are humble, we can be granted a view of things we haven't seen, details and insights that—until now—have escaped us. But note that the scripture doesn't just say Martin had to humble himself; it says he had to humble himself in mighty prayer and faith.

Since faith is an action word, here are a few suggestions of actions that have helped me strive to be humble as I've practiced digging deep.

HUMILITY TIP #1: REJECT NOTHING

Have you ever been in a class where the teacher asks a question that is so obvious that everyone assumes it must be a rhetorical question, and no one raises their hand to answer? It can be tempting to do the same when digging for details; some details seem so obvious, you may not feel they're worth writing. But not writing the first, basic details that come to mind can be as detrimental to your study efforts as *only* writing the first adjectives and moving on.

Excluding a detail for being too basic is in essence saying "the Spirit won't be able to teach me anything insightful with this."

Writing down a word or description, no matter how obvious or basic a detail it may seem, is a way to show humility by admitting that we aren't too good for the basics. We don't know what we don't know, so we can't just assume we already fully understand something. We must allow room in our minds, and on our paper, for the Spirit to teach us about even the most basic of things.

The same principle applies to ideas that seem too obscure. Don't reject them as not being "right" or being too "out there." Write them down. Some of the most interesting insights might come from those mental tangents. And if nothing comes from the obscure detail, it only cost you a few seconds and a tiny bit of space on your list.

HUMILITY TIP #2: ASK QUESTIONS

Asking questions shows humility because we're admitting we don't have answers yet. Here are some questions to consider as we dig for details:

- What are the adjectives and adverbs associated with the nouns and verbs listed as players? (e.g., toothpaste = bright color)
- What does the player do or what is it used for? (e.g., toothpaste = used to clean teeth)
- What is the relationship between this player and the other players? (e.g., crank = turns the gears)
- Are there any conditional aspects or requirements for the player to function? (e.g., crank = must be continually wound)

Other possible questions:

- Why was this word used and not a different one? What characteristics make this object or word different than similar ones that might have been used instead?

- Is this detail an essential characteristic of this player? Why is it essential? How is this characteristic created?

- Is there any aspect of its definition you weren't aware of?

Using the example of our David and Goliath story, we might ask "Why a brook? Why not a river? Or a lake? What makes a brook different than a river or lake?" This could lead us to writing details for brook such as "smaller than a river, constantly flowing water." We might ask "Is smooth an essential characteristic of stones?" This could lead us to ponder how a rough stone won't fly as true when flung from a sling and how the stones being smooth helped David aim them. When we consider how the stones became smooth, we might think of the brook's constantly flowing water and how the steady turbulence chipped away at the stones' rough edges, refining them over a long period of time. And we can write all of that down in the details section.

This kind of systematic study of the relationship between players and deep pondering of the details of their nature can pave the way for a greater payoff when we start likening the players to Christ and ourselves in the next step of the process.

For example, when I was trying to find Christ in the story of David and Goliath, I stopped to ponder that if David represented me and Goliath represented the giant obstacles I face in life, then the stones represented . . . what? They were how David defeated Goliath, which meant that the stones represented whatever I use to defeat the giant obstacles in my life.

I thought of how my faith and testimony, coupled with prayer, allow me to "come off conqueror" (D&C 10:5), and then the Spirit asked me a very important question.

What smooths out my faith?

Because I had pondered the nature of the stones' smoothness, and their relationship not only to David and Goliath, but also to the brook David pulled them from, the Spirit was able to teach me an important lesson. Just as the brook constantly refined the stones, through turbulence, into something smooth that could be aimed with precision, Christ is constantly refining my faith, through trials, into something reliable and sure. If the brook had stopped flowing, the stones might not have been smooth enough to protect David in his moment of need. As much as I might wish for a life of ease, if God removes the constant flow of little trials from my life, my faith might not be sure enough to protect me as I face the bigger trials of mortality.

HUMILITY TIP #3: LOOK UP DEFINITIONS

Looking up definitions for words we already know shows humility because it acknowledges that there might be nuances of the definitions we aren't aware of or hadn't considered. One of the best experiences I've had with this tip was when I studied the iron rod found in Lehi's vision of the tree of life.

The player I was studying was *rod*, and the detail I was trying to dig deep into was *iron*. I asked "Why specify iron? Why not have a rod of gold? Or a plain rod of unspecified composition?" Asking those questions made me wonder "What exactly *is* iron?"

My brain was quick to supply the definition of "a hard, strong metal." Up until that point, this definition of iron had been sufficient for me to make the connection that God's word (which is what 1 Nephi 15:23–24 says the rod represents) is strong and reliable. That was always an easy answer I could check off with confidence, but this time I decided to put in the effort of looking up the definition of iron anyway.

> iron (noun): a silver-white malleable ductile magnetic heavy metallic element that readily rusts in moist air, occurs in pure form in meteorites and combined in most igneous rocks, is the most abundant element on Earth by mass, and is vital to biological processes. (Merriam-Webster online dictionary)

I had been completely wrong about iron being hard and strong! I saw the word *malleable* and began researching the hardness of iron. I learned iron is used to strengthen other materials; when combined with carbon, it creates steel—one of the strongest manmade metals. On its own, however, iron is inherently soft.

I had always thought of the word of God as something hard, something "sharper than a two-edged sword" (D&C 12:2). But thanks to this new definition, I was considering how God's word might also be soft. The hymn "How Gentle God's Commands" came into my mind. I meditated on how much comfort

I get from the word of God and what a tender mercy the commandments truly are.

The insights from this definition didn't stop there. The concept of iron occurring in pure form in meteorites intrigued me. I did more research and learned that iron is rarely ever found on earth in its pure state. It is found abundantly in ores—composites of iron mixed with some other mineral or element—but pure sources of iron are rare and are really only ever found in meteorites that fall from the heavens to the earth.

As soon as I learned this fact about iron, the Spirit taught me the following truth: If you want the pure word of God, check your source. If it's not coming straight from heaven, it may be a diluted form that's been mingled with the philosophies of men.

Write your details in whatever way is the quickest and most comfortable for you.

That iron rod scripture study session is one of my favorite study sessions I've ever had. There is a thrill that comes from having your "understanding enlightened" from a member of the Godhead (see D&C 76:12), a certain rush that comes when you rise from your chair with greater knowledge and faith than when you sat down. I truly believe that all those connections and inspirations I received were only possible because I was humble enough to look up a definition for a word I thought I understood but which clearly contained much more for me to understand.

PRESENTATION OF DETAILS

Now that we've covered how to humbly dig for details, let's talk about how to record them. You can write your details in whatever way works best for you. I prefer a second column next to my list of players, in which I write details in a stream-of-consciousness style. I don't worry about punctuation or spelling or complete sentences. I sometimes abbreviate words or use symbols as shorthand, and if I'm not certain about something, I might include the thought as a question. Some of my details are redundant, but I don't go back and erase them; one phrasing might spark an idea later on that the other wouldn't.

Don't stress about making your details pretty or perfect. The important thing is to get them down. Write your details in whatever way is the quickest and most comfortable for you. As long as you can understand what you wrote when you go back to review your notes, there's no right or wrong way to record your details.

EXAMPLES OF DETAILS: HAND-CRANK FLASHLIGHT

We'll come back to our other two examples (kids making a mess with toothpaste and David and Goliath) in chapter 10, but here is my list of details for our example of a hand-crank flashlight. If you were to make your own list, it might include completely different details than mine, and that's okay. There aren't any specific right answers in this exercise. Just as Christ can be found in all things, you can have insights from any detail.

PLAYERS	DETAILS OF PLAYERS
Hand-crank flashlight	Hand-held, portable, requires someone to crank it Provides light, only shines where pointed, light fades unless consistently cranked
Human	Needs light to see; can function without sight, but not as well (and often not without bumps and bruises) Controls how often the flashlight is cranked and where the light is pointed
Darkness	Lack of light, prohibits sight, conceals potential obstacles, can be scary Vanishes in light, can't overpower light
Light	Reflects off solid objects, making them visible Varying degrees of brightness, even smallest amount dispels darkness Vanishes if power button is switched off Fades gradually if crank isn't rewound
Crank	External feature, turns the gears Different possible styles (handles that spin, triggers) Can be stored flat against the flashlight when not in use
The act of cranking	Requires energy Doesn't have to be continuous, but does need to be consistently repeated
Kinetic energy	Energy created by a body being in motion Can convert to other types of energy

PLAYERS	DETAILS OF PLAYERS
Bulb	Typically LED
	Passes electrical current through semiconductor material, which emits photons, which are visible light
The act of re-cranking	Restores light when it fades, light will disappear without it
	Can get tiresome or annoying to repeat
Reflectors	Reflect the light, typically plastic and aluminum
	Positioned around the bulb, angled to reflect light into one focused beam
Power button	Turns the light off, even when there is stored energy to keep it going
	Must turn on to activate the light
Gears	Turned by the crank
	Transfer the kinetic energy from the human/crank to the generator
Wires	Thin, metal, conduct electricity from generator to battery to bulb
Battery	Stores the energy from the generator and provides power to the flashlight when not actively being cranked
Generator	Converts kinetic energy from gears into electric energy for battery

Before I made this chart, I absolutely did *not* know any of the techy details about flashlights. As I worked on filling out details, I looked up pictures of different styles of hand-crank flashlights and read science tutorials on how to make one or take one apart. By the time I got to reading about what comprises the generator and how it converts energy from one form to the other, I found myself getting overwhelmed by the science. So I stopped.

Remember, stress can be a barrier to feeling the Spirit, so if you're overwhelmed at any step, don't push yourself. Trust that the Spirit will guide you in the process and that God will take whatever you have and—like the loaves and fishes—turn them into something abundantly miraculous.

MATCH TO THE MASTER

"He is above all things, and n all things, and is
through all things, and is round about all things;
and all things are by him, and of him, even God."

DOCTRINE AND COVENANTS 88:41

PLAYING MATCHMAKER

On the eve of my sixteenth birthday, I decided to stay up until
midnight. I sat in front of the mirror, looking at the face of the
fifteen-year-old girl who was "too young to date," anxiously
waiting for that magical moment when I would officially be the
oh-so-datable age of sixteen. Being old enough to date seemed
like such a huge step in my life that I expected it to feel momen-
tous. Instead, it was just a moment. The red digital numbers
on my alarm clock switched from 11:59 to 12:00 without any

fanfare. There was no magical shift inside me. I went to bed feeling silly and more than a bit disappointed, though I consoled myself that the magic would come in the following days when all the eligible boys in my ward started asking me out.

I was almost seventeen before any guy from church asked me on a date, and even then, I suspect it only happened because his mom felt bad for me and paid him to take me to dinner. When he (I'll call him Greg) called to ask me out, he didn't sound enthusiastic at all. Greg was normally pretty quiet, however, so I rationalized that maybe he was just shy and did really like me. Either way, I didn't want to be rude, and I was desperate to go on a date, so I accepted.

We were supposed to double with Greg's best friend and his friend's girlfriend, but the other girl ended up not being able to come. You might think that meant it was just me and Greg, but no. It was me, Greg—the quiet boy who didn't go to the same school as me and hadn't said more than a few sentences to me ever—and Greg's best friend. I sat across the restaurant booth from both boys in what had to be the most painfully awkward dinner date known to puberty.

I kept asking questions, trying to learn more about Greg, but even when he did talk, his short answers revealed that we had nothing in common aside from going to the same church. Our personalities were different, our hobbies and interests were different, even our desire to be on the date in the first place was different. Needless to say, there was no second date.

Flash forward to college, and my dating life finally started picking up. I had one particular friend from institute who I'll call Todd. Todd was tall, cute, charismatic, and kind. I had a *huge* crush on him, and I wasn't the only one. I don't remember if I asked him or somehow convinced him to ask me, but we eventually went on a date, and I was beyond giddy. Todd was polite and as cute as ever, and the date was fun with great conversation. Yet just like the awkward date from high school, I came home knowing that there wouldn't be a second date. Todd was into sports and high-end clothes. I was into books and shopped at Walmart. Despite belonging to the same church, our religious beliefs and priorities didn't quite line up. We were good as friends, but as much as I wanted Todd and me to be a good match, we just didn't have enough in common.

It took me a while, but I did find someone who cared about the things I cared about and had the same priorities I did. Our testimonies were equally strong, our goals for the future aligned, and our senses of humor were so similar that we both told jokes in the same silly voice that everyone called "the voice." Dustin and I had (and still have) our differences, but we had so much in common that when we finally started dating instead of just being best friends, everyone's reaction was simply "it's about time!" I'm happy to report that after almost seventeen years of marriage, we have even more in common and are even better of a match than before.

MATCHING TO THE MASTER

While we aren't trying to play matchmaker in a romantic sense, finding symbols that match Christ follows the same principle— for it to be a good match, both parties must have something in common. To begin making connections between the players we've listed and the Savior, we're going to read through all the attributes we listed in our details column and pay attention to any that match what we know about Christ and His attributes.

If you're struggling to find any details that match Christ as a person, try shifting your search to look for things associated with His mission and role in our lives: Christ's gospel, Christ's Atonement, Christ's commandments, Christ's love, etc. Sometimes Christ feels so broad and expansive, we need something more specific to jumpstart our ideas and connections.

With our hand-crank flashlight, the details that match what I know about the Savior's attributes include:

- dispels darkness (light)
- emits light (bulb)
- restores (the act of re-cranking)
- provides power (battery)

We could pick any of these details to explore as a symbol of Christ, and over the course of this chapter we will explore more than one, but to start, let's go with the first one on this list. Christ is like light because he dispels the darkness in our lives.

WHERE AM I?

When I was called to teach seminary and learned I'd be teaching the Old Testament, one book in particular intimidated me more than all the others—Isaiah. Due to its abundant symbolism and use of historical and cultural ideas that are often unfamiliar to modern readers, the book of Isaiah has a reputation for being difficult to understand. I understood some of it, but I definitely didn't feel like I understood it enough to teach it so simply that even a bunch of sleep-deprived teens could understand.

Thankfully, I was able to learn from teachers far better than me. Part of my calling as a seminary teacher included regular training meetings from CES professionals, and knowing the apprehension many of us might have about teaching the book of Isaiah, they devoted an entire training meeting to helping us understand it. I can't remember the name of the brother who was teaching that training, but I'll never forget what he taught.

If Christ is here, then where am I?

He said that there were three key questions that would make every chapter in Isaiah easier to understand.

1. When is the chapter referring to? (Most of Isaiah refers to either the fall of Jerusalem, Christ's mortal ministry, the restoration and gathering of Israel, or Christ's Second Coming and the Millennium.)
2. What words or names do I need to research to understand the context?
3. Where is Christ in this passage, and where am I?

That third question forever changed the way I look at all scripture, not just the book of Isaiah. It seemed so simple, yet profound. Finding Christ in the scriptures is important, but so is finding ourselves. However, I've taken that question one step further. Once we've found a player that shares at least one or more characteristics with Christ, our next objective in this process is to ask "If Christ is here, then where am I?"

Our goal is to better understand Christ *and our relationship to Him.*

The if-then relationship in that question is key. We could simply look through the list of details and find one that matches Christ and another that matches us, but that's not the purpose of this kind of mental exercise and spiritual study session. Our goal is to better understand Christ *and our relationship to Him,* so instead of simply identifying any random player you share a characteristic with, focus on the relationship between the player you've matched to the Master and the one you're comparing to yourself.

Looking at our flashlight example, if light is a symbol for the Savior, then what are we?

The obvious choice would be the human, so let's start there and see what insights we can glean about our relationship with Christ. Here are the details under *human* from our chart at the end of the last chapter:

- Needs light to see
- Can function without sight, but not as well (and often not without bumps and bruises)
- Controls how often the flashlight is cranked and where the light is pointed

If we substitute "Christ" for anytime we used the word *light* (or sight, which is made possible because of light), we'll get statements like these:

- Needs Christ to see
- Can function without Christ (or at least without acknowledging Him), but not as well (and often not without bumps and bruises)
- Controls how often the flashlight is cranked and where Christ is pointed

Does that feel like an accurate parallel to our relationship with Christ? The first two statements for sure. Christ helps us see things as they really are, and while we can live our lives without Him, there will be a lot of otherwise-avoidable bumps and bruises along the way.

What about that last statement though? Do we control where Christ is pointed? It feels odd to think that we control Christ, but what if we rephrase the original wording of "controls where the light is pointed" with "controls what areas the light illuminates"?

Does that feel accurate now? Do we control what areas of our lives Christ can illuminate? Are there certain aspects of our lives we are fine letting Him into while trying to keep Him out of other areas?

For me, there's truth there. Christ stands at the door and knocks (Revelation 3:20). He won't barge into any areas of my life I'm not willing to open the door and let Him into.

Now, I realize that the idea of Christ being symbolized by light isn't anything new. The Psalmist wrote, "The Lord is my light and my salvation" (Psalm 27:1), and Christ Himself said, "I am come a light into the world" (John 12:46).

The value in this Christ-finding exercise, however, doesn't lie in finding something to compare Christ to that you've never thought of before. The value of this exercise comes from focusing on the relationship between the symbols you've found for Him and yourself.

I have sung "The Lord Is My Light" more times than I can remember, but each time I've only thought about Christ as a general light illuminating my whole life. Now, thanks to that detail I wrote about a how a human can control where the light of the hand-crank flashlight points. I'm pondering if perhaps there are specific parts of my life I might not be letting Christ into—if there are parts of my life I'm choosing to keep dark. It's something I hadn't considered before, but I'm grateful to be considering now.

MATCHING OTHER PLAYERS

Now that we've matched players to ourselves as well as Christ, we can ponder our relationship to Him even more by considering what other players in the subject might symbolize. For example, we've said the light symbolizes Christ and the human symbolizes us. If that's the case, what about the act of re-cranking? Our details for the act of re-cranking include:

- Restores light when it fades
- Light will disappear without it
- Can get tiresome or annoying to repeat

Is there an action we can take that restores Christ to our lives? How do we repeat that re-cranking action to strengthen His influence in our lives?

There are lots of valid answers. Prayer, scripture study, and repentance can all restore our relationship with Christ and be frequently repeated to strengthen His influence in our lives. There's also the renewal of our baptismal covenants through weekly participation in the sacrament.

When my youngest son was old enough to walk, my husband was in the bishopric. I spent the entirety of sacrament meeting chasing my toddler up and down the aisles of the chapel, trying to keep him from running up to where Daddy was, all the while hoping my three other kids were behaving on the pew. When sacrament meeting ended, I often spent the rest of church in the halls with the baby, since he wasn't old enough for nursery and my husband had more obligations with his calling. When Dustin *was* able to take the baby, I spent my time trying to manage other small kids as a member of the Primary presidency. And since we only had one car, I was often waiting in the foyer for an hour after church, trying to keep all four kids entertained while Daddy had tithing duties or other meetings.

Church was exhausting. I didn't feel like I was getting anything out of it most weeks. I felt spiritually drained when we came home from church, not spiritually renewed. I took the sacrament, but that was about all I got out of the weekly experience, and it was often a hurried, perfunctory action—a quick chew and swallow where my thoughts were often centered not on Christ but on keeping the tray from my baby's grabbing hands as I whispered to get my other kids' attention so they could take the tray and pass it on.

And yet, I still went. Week after week.

As I ponder how the act of going to church and taking the sacrament is like re-cranking the flashlight, I realize that any amount of re-cranking helps recharge the light. An amazing spiritual experience every week at church would be like an extended, vigorous cranking session, one that really brightens the overall beam. But even an exhausted experience at church, one where all I could do was swallow the sacrament and support my husband in his callings, was at least one revolution of the crank. It might not have strengthened my faith in Christ the way I wanted, but it kept Christ in my life enough that I had what it took to drag myself to church each week.

I can't speak for anyone else facing spiritual depletion from caregiver burnout, but I can testify that as I pondered the idea of what a single revolution of the crank might do, the Spirit confirmed to me that in my case, if I had stopped going to church until things got easier, I would have risked the light fading from my life completely.

Pondering the value of a single turn of the crank when vigorous cranking isn't possible has strengthened my relationship with Christ. It's helped me think about other ways He magnifies my meager efforts and sustains me when I am weak. And that is the purpose behind exploring the other players outside of your primary pairings.

REIMAGINE THE MATCHES

Now let's try choosing a different symbol for Christ. Instead of comparing Christ to the light and us to the human, let's say Christ is the bulb that emits lights and we are the reflectors—things that are typically made from weak materials, yet when they are positioned around the bulb and angled correctly they can reflect the light into a stronger, more focused beam.

Christ said, "If men come unto me I will show unto them their weakness. I give unto men weakness that they may be humble; and my grace is sufficient for all men that humble themselves before me; for if they humble themselves before me, and have faith in me, then will I make weak things become strong unto them" (Ether 12:27).

So no matter how imperfect (made of weak materials) we feel we are, if we come unto Christ (position ourselves around the bulb) and humble ourselves (angle ourselves correctly), He will give us the strength to be like Him, to reflect His light more powerfully than before (reflecting the light into a stronger more focused beam).

But what if the reflectors aren't angled correctly? What if we position ourselves around Christ (for example, join His Church) yet lack the humility to bend our will to His? What kind of example would we create for others if we profess to have Christ at the center of our lives yet don't do the things necessary to reflect His light?

There are more questions we could ask to explore the relationship between this bulb/reflector pairing, but there's just as much to ponder in that relationship as there is with the light/human pairing. It might be tempting to worry about which pairing is right or better, but any number of pairings can be equally edifying. Remember that in the scriptures Christ is compared to both the Good Shepherd (John 10:14) and the Lamb of God (John 1:29), and both are wonderful comparisons that teach us different things about Christ and His relationship to us.

So once you've found a symbolic pairing that gives you insight, consider going back, whether right then or in a future study session, to look for more potential matches. Hold your subject up to the light and examine it from a different angle. You may be surprised just how much the Spirit can teach you.

KNOW YOUR TARGET

What if you can't find Christ? What if, after reading all the details of all the players, none of them jump out at you as matching the Master?

Like we did with the phrase about controlling where the light points, you can try rephrasing your details to see if that sparks any ideas. One of the details listed for the flashlight as a whole is "portable," but that's not a description I usually associate with Christ. However, if "portable" is rephrased as "able to go with me anywhere," my thoughts instantly turn to the promise in the sacrament prayers that I can "always have his Spirit to be with [me]" (D&C 20:77). The hand-crank flashlight as a whole didn't make my initial list of potential symbols for Christ, but after reframing that idea of portability, I can say that just as a hand-crank flashlight is portable, Christ's Spirit is able to be with me anywhere I go.

While rephrasing your attributes can help, the best thing you can do when you're struggling to find Christ is to learn more about Him. The more we know about the nature and mission of Christ, the easier it will be to recognize His attributes in the various players of our subjects.

The wealth of resources available to us for learning about Christ are so numerous, it can be difficult to know where to begin, so here are a few of my favorite ways to learn more about Christ:

- Read the four Gospels of the New Testament and make specific notes of how He interacted with His disciples and apostles.

- Make a list of the promises He made in the Old Testament.

- Compare every prophecy Isaiah made about the Savior with the scripture that fulfills it.

- Study the chapter "How Do I Develop Christlike Attributes?" in the *Preach My Gospel* manual.

- Review the document "The Living Christ: The Testimony of the Apostles."

- Go through the hymnbook and make a list of every adjective used to describe the Savior or His Atonement.

- Pray. Tell Heavenly Father why you desire to understand Christ's attributes better. Stay on your knees afterward to listen.

As you learn more about Christ, consider compiling a list or database with everything you know about Him—all the names He's given and the adjectives and verbs associated with Him. The act of writing down the attributes in the database will make them easier to recall during later studies, and if you alphabetize your list or use a software with a search feature, finding matching attributes will be that much easier if your memory isn't cooperating.

WORK-AROUNDS

While I recommend first trying to match a symbol to Christ (since He should always be our focus), if you find yourself unable to draw a parallel between Christ and any of the players in your chosen subject, try matching a player to yourself instead. Once you've found yourself in the subject material, study the remaining players and how they relate to the one you matched to yourself to see if a connection to Christ stands out.

With our flashlight example, let's say you didn't see a connection between Christ and any of the players. Perhaps every time you read the details associated with light, you thought of how Christ said, "Ye are the light of the world" (Matthew 5:14), and you saw light as a symbol of yourself.

From there, you could ask "If I am the light, what would Christ be?"

If that still doesn't help you identify a match for Christ, try asking "If I am the light, what could [insert the name of another player] represent?"

You might also ask relationship questions about the nature of the symbol you've matched to yourself, such as "What creates the light?" or "Who benefits from the light?"

You could even start with something you already know about your relationship with Christ and work backward with questions such as "Christ sacrificed Himself for me. What sacrifices itself for the light?" or "I rely on Christ to strengthen me. What does the light rely on for strength?"

You may have to expand your list of players to find the one that best fits Christ in relationship to the symbol you've chosen for yourself. But if you find one symbol to start with and keep pondering the relationships between that player and all the others, eventually, you will find your way to Christ.

As long as you're pondering your relationship with Christ, the exercise is a success.

In the case of our flashlight, matching yourself to the light and asking what creates the light could lead you to saying that just as the human creates the light, Christ (along with the Father) created you. Now that you have players matched to both you and Christ, you can dig into the other players and create more symbolic connections to help you think more deeply about your relationship with Christ.

For example, re-cranking. If a human can continually re-crank the flashlight to create more light, how can Christ continually create "more" of us—how can He ensure, as Paul said it, that our "inward man is renewed day by day" (2 Corinthians 4:16)?

Whether you start with finding Christ, yourself, or any other comparison the Spirit gives you first, as long as you end up pondering the relationship between yourself and Christ, the exercise is a success.

A CAUTIONARY TALE FROM THE ROAD TO EMMAUS

Sometimes there will be an obvious correlation between a player in your subject and the Savior (e.g., light = Christ). Exploring those obvious matches can yield spiritually profitable insights, but don't be afraid to look for Him in the seemingly less likely matches as well. Consider Cleopas and his companion walking on the road to Emmaus after Christ's death and Resurrection (Luke 24:13–35).

The resurrected Lord appeared, walked with them, and talked about the scriptures with them. Their hearts burned with the Spirit as they listened. However, they didn't recognize Him.

The scriptures say that "their eyes were holden that they should not know him" (Luke 24:16), meaning they were prevented from recognizing Him. What the scriptures don't say, however, is who or what was doing the preventing. It could be that God, for some divine purpose, caused them to not realize who they were with at first. But I think it's also likely that their eyes were prevented from recognizing Christ by their own limited sense of what was possible or likely.

The Christ they knew was dead. True, there had been rumors and reports of His Resurrection, but it still seemed too fantastic, too impossible to consider searching for Him in the face of the man who walked beside them. The unlikelihood of it was so profound in their minds that it blocked out the burning of their hearts, which was trying to confirm the Savior was right there with them.

It wasn't until they saw Christ blessing and breaking bread before them that their eyes were opened, and they finally recognized Him. They might not have been witness to the Last Supper, but they could have heard all about it from the apostles during the time between Christ's death and Resurrection. As Christ's disciples, they very likely could have been in the crowd of five thousand and watched Him bless and break the bread and fish that would miraculously feed them all. For whatever reason, this act of breaking bread was familiar, something they already associated with Christ, and it helped them recognize Christ in the stranger before them.

How wonderful that they finally saw Him; their testimonies must have swelled in that moment. However, He had been there all along. How much greater their joy could have been if instead of waiting for the familiar idea of Him to manifest itself, they had been open to the possibility of recognizing Him where they least expected to find Him.

FORWARD
WITH FAITH

"For I the Lord thy God will hold thy right hand,
saying unto thee, Fear not; I will help thee."

ISAIAH 41:13

I've noticed some recurring fears and concerns people often have regarding this process of delving into the world of symbols. Since fear hinders faith, and this Christ-finding process only works through faith, I'd like to address a few of those fears and hopefully help you avoid them.

WHAT IF I COME UP WITH A WRONG COMPARISON?

One of the biggest hurdles I see with people trying to find their own symbols is the fear of getting it wrong. Because of this fear, some people might not try to find symbols at all, relying instead on teachers or church manuals to tell them A is a symbol for B. Others might try to find their own symbols but dismiss a thought that comes to them because it "sounds silly."

In my experience, "sounds silly" is a shorthand way of saying "it's something I haven't heard anyone else say, and I don't have the confidence to be the first to say it because if I don't get it right, I'm afraid I will be judged by others."

This fear of being wrong or sounding silly extends to so many aspects of our lives. I remember one fall day in Minnesota, after dropping one kid off at school and heading to another school for the third drop-off of the morning, I passed a home with a sheriff's car and ambulance in the driveway. Behind the ambulance was a stretcher with a body on it, covered in a white sheet. I only caught a fleeting glimpse as I drove by, but my heart was touched at what a sad morning it must be for whoever had lost a loved one. Then I had a quick thought that I should bring them flowers.

The problem was I had no idea who lived there. Just thinking about showing up at some stranger's house and intruding on their very personal life made me feel silly. So I pushed aside the idea and went about my day. As luck (or the Spirit) would have it, my day soon involved running over a screw, getting a flat tire, and going to Costco to see if they could fix it.

You know what else they have at Costco? Fresh flower bouquets at prices I could actually afford.

I don't know how long I stood in front of their flower stand, trying to decide between sunflowers, daisies, and an arrangement of autumn-colored blooms, all the while feeling ridiculous.

I was not prepared for the excruciatingly awkward moment of knocking on a stranger's door just to hand them flowers and say, "Hey, looks like someone died. Sorry.'

I pushed through those feelings by remembering that it would be a kind gesture and I should never suppress a kind thought no matter how silly or awkward it might make me feel to carry it out. So I bought the daisies, drove my now screw-free car to the now ambulance-free home, and knocked on the front door.

No one answered, and I was so relieved.

I had a pen and paper in the car and was planning to leave an anonymous note, but when I turned to head back to the car, a short, thin gentleman that looked to be in his sixties or seventies had come out the side door of the house and was looking at me expectantly. So much for leaving a nice note and avoiding the awkward greeting.

I took a deep breath and blurted out one of the world's most ineloquent introductions.

"Hi. I was passing your house this morning after taking my kids to school and noticed a sheriff's car and an ambulance and what looked like a body on a stretcher with a sheet over it, and did somebody die?"

He cocked an eyebrow, looking at me like I'd just stepped off a UFO, and said, "No."

I had gotten it wrong—no one had died. All my fears of feeling silly were realized in that instant, and I was so embarrassed, I couldn't even form words to apologize for my misunderstanding.

But then he continued talking. "My mom fell. It was a bad one. She's ninety-three. The bone was practically breaking through the skin. She's at the hospital now with my brothers in surgery."

"Oh," I said. "Well . . . I'm glad it wasn't something worse, but I know that's still a hard ordeal. So, these are for you." I awkwardly held out the flowers. "Or . . . her."

He took the flowers from me, and the next thing I knew, he was hugging me with tears in his eyes. After a moment of shock, all my feelings of awkwardness melted, and I hugged him back. We cried together. It was a beautifully poignant moment of shared humanity.

And it never would have happened if I'd let my fears of feeling silly keep me from pursuing an idea.

None of us wants to feel silly or get things wrong, but one of the best parts of this Christ-finding process is that you don't have to be embarrassed about not knowing the right answer because there is no one right answer. There's only inspiration that is right for you, right at this moment. There are so many aspects of truth to be pondered, so many possible right answers, that a "right vs. wrong" line of thinking is dangerous. This process isn't about trying to find *the* right answer. It is about pondering long enough and frequently enough that the Spirit can teach us line upon line about Christ, thus deepening

> **There's nothing wrong with exploring an avenue of thought and then deciding it doesn't work.**

our understanding of things we think we understand but which, in reality, we only "know in part" (1 Corinthians 13:12).

Are there wrong answers? Perhaps. But don't assume a match is wrong just because it's not an obvious answer. There can be hidden gems of insight in the least likely of symbol pairings.

Do assume, however, that if something isn't a good match, the Spirit will let you know. Have confidence in the Spirit's ability to teach and instruct you in the way you learn best. If a match or relationship doesn't feel right, simply move on. There's nothing wrong with exploring an avenue of thought and then deciding it doesn't work. You were only following Paul's counsel to "prove all things" and then "hold fast that which is good" (1 Thessalonians 5:21).

So if your first ideas don't feel right, let them go without judgement and keep searching for a symbol that fits better—a parallel relationship where the Spirit confirms to your heart and your mind, "Yes. This is true. This is what you need to know right now."

The bottom line is if your thoughts are centering on Christ and if you're pondering your relationship to Him or gaining any kind of insights during the process, you are doing it right.

I FEEL LIKE I'M JUST MAKING STUFF UP

Another concern people express is that they aren't sure if the thoughts they have and connections they make during this process are actual revelation or if it's just their brain connecting the dots however it wants. I used to struggle with this idea myself, unable to distinguish between mere good ideas and thoughts that were inspired of God. My answer came as I was studying in the Book of Mormon, in Moroni 7:13: "But behold, that which is of God inviteth and enticeth to do good continually; wherefore, every thing which inviteth and enticeth to do good, and to love God, and to serve him, is inspired of God."

It's a perfect litmus test for revelation and inspiration. If the idea you're having is in line with the doctrines you know, if it points your soul to Christ, if it fills you with gratitude for what He's done for you, or if it reminds you of what you need to do for Him, that idea is inspired. Sometimes we get so accustomed to the presence of the Spirit in our lives, we don't recognize it all the time. We wait for some spectacular revelation to burn our hearts and shake us to our core, but as Elijah learned, "The Lord was not in the wind: and after the wind an earthquake; but the Lord was not in the earthquake: And after the earthquake a fire; but the Lord was not in the fire: and after the fire a still small voice" (1 Kings 19:11–12).

Back in chapter 7, I shared a scripture study experience I had regarding the concept of the iron rod and many of the insights that came from researching iron as an element and mineral. Another insight I had during that study session was that the periodic symbol for iron is "Fe," which also happens to be the Spanish word for faith.

Now, did Lehi know about this iron = Fe = faith connection when he had his vision of the rod and specified that it was an iron rod? I'm confident he didn't. Lehi had his vision around 600 BC. While Latin as a language began about 100 years prior to that, the development of the Spanish language (based on a spoken Latin dialect) didn't occur until around 300 BC, long after Lehi's death. It would be another two thousand years before Swedish scientist J. J. Berzelius, in 1813, would propose the idea to use chemical symbols based on the Latin names of each element. The fact that Fe is both a Latin-derived symbol for iron as well as the Spanish word for faith is pure coincidence, one that didn't even exist when Lehi had his original vision.

Just because a certain message wasn't intended by the original author, however, doesn't mean the message isn't a valid one coming from the Spirit right now.

When I realized the coincidental Fe connection, my thoughts went like this: If iron is faith, and if the iron rod is the word of God, then how is faith an element of the word of God? As I pondered the role between faith and God's word, the Spirit whispered to me that Christ is the Word (John 1:1), and there is no true faith but in Him.

How can I be sure those thoughts were whisperings of the Spirit and not just my own ideas? After all, the Joseph Smith translation for John 1:1 doesn't say "the Word was God," but rather "the gospel was the word, and the word was with the Son, and the Son was with God, and the Son was of God" (John 1:1, footnote a).

Christ wants to be found.

I can be sure because thinking about the coincidental Fe connection led me to thinking about how true faith is centered on Christ, which enticed me to love and serve God and to have faith in Him. According to Mormon's litmus test, that means my thought about the Fe connection was inspired by God, even if that connection was coincidental and never originally intended by its author.

So have faith. Work the process, and don't worry about getting things wrong. Christ-finding is not a test; it's a process of developing a relationship. It's putting in the effort to always remember Christ by training your brain to find symbols of Him all around you. I promise that as you put in the effort, He will be an active part of that relationship as well. He wants to be found. Trust that the Spirit will guide your heart and mind to the symbols of Him that are right for you at this time in your life. Let your brain explore whatever thoughts come, no matter how silly, simple, or coincidental they may first seem to be.

WHAT IF MY IDEA FOR A SYMBOL DOESN'T MATCH EVERY DETAIL OF THE SUBJECT I'M MATCHING IT TO?

When we owned our own home in Arizona, I was determined to grow a small vegetable garden. I had never grown anything before and wasn't sure if I could do it, but I went ahead and bought an assortment of seeds and did as much research as one could do by reading the back of the seed packet. I don't remember every type of seed I planted, but I do remember the carrots. I couldn't believe how small and paper-thin those carrot seeds were.

Following the packet's instructions, I sprinkled the seeds in rows, covered them in dirt, and watered them regularly. After a couple weeks, to my utter excitement, little narrow blades of green were shooting up from the dirt where my carrots had been planted. My other crops were growing much more slowly, so my carrots helped maintain my enthusiasm. I loved going out each day and seeing those single blades start to leaf out on top. Before I knew it, that whole section of my garden bed was covered in feathery green bunches, and I took joy in this obvious testament to my horticultural capabilities.

Now, the seed packet had also said I should thin out the crop once the leafy tops were a few inches tall, but obviously the people who wrote those instructions had never seen carrot tops as cute as the ones I was growing. I was so proud to actually be growing something that the idea of committing baby carrot murder by destroying any of my little green victories was unbearable. So I left them in the soil and continued watering and caring for them all, basking in the joy of watching those green stems and leafy tops grow larger and larger.

When harvest time finally came, however, my joy vanished. To my dismay, instead of fat crunchy carrots, all I pulled out were massive clumps of thin, tangled, orange strings. The carrots were all so scrawny and knotted together that none of them could be used. I should have committed to only the best and strongest carrots. By not weeding out the smaller ones and giving the remaining ones sufficient room to grow straight and true, I lost the usefulness of them all.

Because there is no way of knowing beforehand which seeds will grow, or which will grow best, the process of over-seeding (planting more than you need) and later weeding out any excess is a long-standing gardening principle. This same principle applies to our symbolic Christ-finding process as well.

The goal is to come up with more players and details than you can use. Plant them all by writing them on the page. This is your way of overseeding. Once you start matching attributes and making comparisons, certain details and players will be a strong fit, while others won't seem to match at all. When that happens, focus on the strong matches, and weed out all the rest. You don't have to fit every player or every detail into the same comparison. Trying to do so will only turn each symbolic comparison you come up with into a tangled, unusable mess.

If you can match at least one detail of one player to Christ and one detail of another player to yourself while learning something about your relationship with the Savior in the process, then your Christ-finding garden is a success.

ISN'T IT A BIT BLASPHEMOUS TO COMPARE IMPERFECT THINGS TO CHRIST?

Hens poop everywhere and bathe in dirt. Bread often gets moldy or stale. Adam transgressed the law of God and brought death to the world. But do you know what all these things have in common? They're all used as symbols of Christ in the scriptures (see Matthew 23:37, John 6:35, and Romans 5:14).

Their imperfect qualities are not the details being matched to Christ; they're the little carrot sprouts you have to weed out so you can focus on the other attributes that *do* apply to Christ.

The law of Moses was described as "having a shadow of good things to come, and not the very image of the things" (Hebrews 10:1). When we look for types and shadows of Christ, we aren't attempting to perfectly replicate the very image of Him. He is, after all, the *Only* Begotten. No one and nothing will ever perfectly compare to Him who is perfect. When we make our comparisons, we are merely using them to pull our focus to the Savior, thus deepening our faith and relationship with Him.

A shadow by its very definition isn't perfect. According to Merriam-Webster online dictionary, a shadow is "an imperfect and faint representation."

Imagine yourself facing a blank wall. The room you're in is dark except for a single light directly behind you. As your body blocks some of the light from reaching the wall, you create a shadow. With the light source directly behind you, your shadow will be a pretty accurate representation of your true shape. But what if the light source moved higher, lower, or to the side? Your shadow would lengthen and distort. It would become an imperfect representation of your true form, but it would still be your shadow.

The same is true for every shadow of Christ. Imperfections are expected, not invalidating.

ISN'T THIS A BIT OF A STRETCH?

This concern encompasses a lot of what we've already discussed, but it bears repeating. As we practice finding shared characteristics between our Savior and the everyday objects and occurrences around us, some things will feel like a stretch. That's okay. The point isn't to find the perfect thing whose every aspect represents Christ, but rather, to find a piece of Christ represented in everything.

If your idea seems silly or a bit of a stretch, ask yourself "Does this idea contradict any revealed doctrines? Is it pointing me toward Christ and reminding me of His love or expectations of me?"

If you can answer no to the first question and yes to the second, then your thought is inspired of God, according to Mormon's litmus test in Moroni 7:13. Rest assured that you're on the right track, no matter how silly your comparisons may seem. Go forward with faith and let the Spirit edify you.

There is no one right answer. There's just inspiration that is right for you, right at this moment.

GUIDED PRACTICE

"And he said, How can I, except some man should
guide me?"

ACTS 8:31

KIDS MAKING A MESS
WITH TOOTHPASTE

DIG FOR DETAILS

The following chart contains our previously listed players from
our kids and toothpaste scenario, along with the details I came
up with for each player. In making my list of details, some of
the things I considered included adjectives and adverbs associated with the players, the function and purpose of each
player, required conditions for players to function properly, the

relationship between players, each player's essential characteristics, and why those characteristics are essential.

The presentation doesn't have to be pretty, and redundant ideas are fine. My list may look completely different than anyone else's (and be twice as long), and that's fine too. All we're doing at this point is listing a bunch of attributes that will hopefully trigger at least one parallel to Christ in the next phase of this process.

PLAYERS	DETAILS OF PLAYERS
Kids	Young, still learning, limited experience, less strength and hand-eye coordination
	Playful, easily distracted
	Only responsible for themselves
Adults	Older, responsible for kids (and self, house, etc.), more experience and strength
	Often more tired, less playful
Bathroom	Necessary room, everyone needs to use it
	Lots of germ potential
	Has sinks, counters, bathtub, toilet, mirrors, tiled floor, and rugs
Mess	Not supposed to be there, ugly, sticky
	Can spread if not cleaned quickly
	Wastes toothpaste

PLAYERS	DETAILS OF PLAYERS
Toothpaste	Soft, squeezable (until it dries out, then it gets hard); easy to squeeze out too much
	Goes on toothbrush
	Helps fight bacteria and keep teeth healthy; brushing without it doesn't clean teeth as well
	Relatively inexpensive
	Bright blue (kids' version)
Toothpaste tube	Holds toothpaste; can't see inside to view amount remaining
	Either has a flip top or a screw-on cap; narrow opening to dispense
	Once toothpaste comes out, it can't go back in
Lid to the toothpaste tube	Screw-on lids = small and easily lost
	Difficult to get back on if there's excess toothpaste around the opening
The act of squeezing out too much	Happens more when the tube is full
	Can't put excess back in tube
	Happens if you aren't paying attention or don't know how to regulate the amount of pressure you squeeze with
The act of squeezing from the bottom	Keeps the toothpaste toward the top
	Aids in using all the toothpaste
	Not where you instinctively want to squeeze from; learned technique

PLAYERS	DETAILS OF PLAYERS
The act of believing there's no toothpaste left	Happens when you squeeze and nothing comes out
	More common when tube is mangled from squeezing in random places instead of from bottom
	Can't see inside tube to know for certain
The act of wandering around or goofing off	Sometimes intentional, other times not
	Often triggered by boredom
Extra tubes of toothpaste	Previously purchased by parent
	Kept nearby for easy use; not needed until previous tube runs out
	Starts out full, with new cap and pristine top
	No limit to how many you can buy
Cleaning supplies	Used to remove messes and germs
	Different messes require different cleaners
	Purchased and made available by parents
Pain	Uncomfortable, undesirable
	Can override other sensations and emotions as well as logic
Teeth	Hard, but subject to decay
	White, but can yellow without cleaning
	Used to chew and talk
	Baby teeth fall out, replaced by permanent teeth; losing teeth doesn't happen all at once

PLAYERS	DETAILS OF PLAYERS
Hand-eye coordination	Learned skill that mproves with age
Patience	Good to have, allows space for grace, often runs short at end of day. Requires mental energy and control
	No one makes you lose it; you control whether you lose or keep
	Ability to tolerate delays or hardships without getting angry
Experience	Understanding gained by doing something
	Can't be transferred from one person to another; only way to get it is to live it yourself
	More time alive = more experience

LIST THE POSSIBLE MASTER MATCHES

The next step is to scan through our list of details and make note of anything that reminds us of Christ. If necessary, we can reword details to make them more widely applicable. For example, with this list of details, we could reword "bacteria" as "destructive forces."

The matches you find might lock different than mine, but here are the key words and ideas I found that could match what I know of Christ or His Atonement:

- Responsible for others, older, more experience (adult)
- Everyone needs to use it (bathroom)
- Helps fight destructive forces, relatively inexpensive (toothpaste)
- Aids in maximizing what you can get (the act of squeezing from the bottom)
- New, full, pristine, no limit to how many you can use (extra tubes of toothpaste)
- Used to remove messes (cleaning supplies)
- Allows for grace, you control whether you lose or keep (patience)

PICK A MATCH FOR CHRIST

The possible match that got my brain percolating the most was the idea of having no limit to how many extra tubes of toothpaste I could use. The idea of limitless fresh starts really resonates with what I know about Christ's Atonement. In speaking of the Church after Christ's visit to the Americas, Moroni wrote, "But as oft as they repented and sought forgiveness, with real intent, they were forgiven" (Moroni 6:8). Christ provides us limitless chances to repent, to renew our baptismal covenants, to walk in "newness of life" (Romans 6:4). A new tube of toothpaste every time we need one.

The more I pondered this idea, however, the more I realized Christ's Atonement isn't the extra tubes of toothpaste. The extra tubes would represent a clean slate or perfectly clean life. Christ's Atonement is how He provides those extra tubes.

It doesn't matter if you find Christ first, last, or somewhere along the way. Finding Him is all that matters.

TYPES, SHADOWS, AND CASSEROLES

Which brings me to an important point: it's okay if the original thing you intended to match to Christ winds up connecting to something else instead. All you're looking for is a way in, some connection to spark ideas and provide a path for the Spirit to teach you. In pondering the symbolism, it doesn't matter if you find Christ first, last, or somewhere along the way. Finding Him is all that matters, and whatever mental route takes you to Him is the one you need to be on.

If life is a tube of toothpaste, and Christ's Atonement is the means by which He provides limitless new tubes (clean slates in life), then what would Christ be in this analogy?

He would be the adult or parent, the one providing the toothpaste in the first place.

IF CHRIST IS HERE, WHERE AM I?

Now that we've found Christ, the next step is to find ourselves in relation to Him.

Continuing with our previous pairing, if Christ is the adult or parent continually providing fresh new tubes of toothpaste, then we would be the kids—the ones He continually offers the renewed chances to. And if we are the kids and life is the toothpaste, then the title of this example could swap from "kids making a mess with toothpaste" to "me making a mess of my life."

For me, that rings with more truth than I like to admit. How grateful I am for a Savior who continually offers me the supplies I need to clean up my messes and a fresh start every time I mess up.

MATCHING ADDITIONAL PLAYERS

So we have Christ as the parent, us as the kids, life as the toothpaste, and Christ's Atonement as the limitless supply of extra tubes provided for us. We've found Christ, we've found ourselves, and we've pondered a little about our relationship with Christ.

We could stop here, feeling gratitude for Christ's Atonement in our lives. If that's all we have time for, we should feel good about our efforts; we've succeeded in pondering Christ and feeling the Spirit. Since we have more time, however, let's keep matching other elements to see what more we can learn about our relationship with Christ.

We've mentioned that the mess kids make with toothpaste is like the mess we might make with our lives. We get ourselves in places we're not supposed to be, in sticky situations we don't know how to get out of. Sin seems like a good summary for all of that. So what can we learn from our toothpaste example about our relationship to sin?

What can you remove from your life in order to stay spiritually regulated?

Looking back at our initial subject, what caused the mess to happen was wandering around or goofing off and squeezing out too much toothpaste. If we examine the details of those two players, there are all kinds of insights we might get.

Take the act of wandering around or goofing off, for example. The details say *sometimes intentional, other times not* and *often triggered by boredom*.

Here are some questions we might ask ourselves:

127

- Which sins do I choose intentionally? Why do I choose them?

- Which of my frequent sins happen unintentionally, and how can I prevent them?

- Do I ever get bored with living the gospel? If boredom is the result of having nothing to do and lacking interest, then how might church callings or other service help keep me from being bored? How might fulfilling a calling or serving others keep me from sinning?

The details for squeezing out too much toothpaste include *happens more when the tube is full, can't put excess back in tube,* and *happens if you aren't paying attention or don't know how to regulate the amount of pressure you squeeze with.*

Those details make me wonder: Am I more likely to stray and sin when my life feels too full? Which pressures do I need in my life? What expectations, habits, or other things can I remove from my life in order to stay spiritually regulated?

King Benjamin taught, "It is not requisite that a man should run faster than he has strength" (Mosiah 4:27). If we try to run faster or squeeze more out of our lives than we have the means to safely give, we'll wind up with a mess. Applying no pressure at all isn't the answer; we need to challenge ourselves and grow. Life is meant to be lived, but if we want to live it cleanly, and we don't want to waste any of it, we need to do things in "wisdom and order" as King Benjamin taught in that same verse.

What about the act of squeezing from the bottom of the tube? The original details I came up with are *keeps the toothpaste toward the top, aids in using all the toothpaste,* and *not where you instinctively want to squeeze from; learned technique.* To me, that symbolizes living the gospel. Living according to Christ's gospel doesn't come instinctively or naturally. After all, "the natural man is an enemy to God" (Mosiah 3 19). Yet we can learn to live by Christ's gospel, and doing so will keep us moving forward and help us get the most out of life. As Christ taught, "I am come that they might have life, and that they might have it more abundantly" (John 10:10).

We could keep going with all kinds of other matches in our Christ = adult and we = kids pairing. We could even reimagine the matches if we wanted, picking new players to symbolize either Christ or ourselves. For the sake of this book, however, I'll close this particular example with one final question I want you to ponder on your own:

If squeezing from the bottom represents living the gospel, what could be represented by the act of believing there's no toothpaste left?

DAVID AND GOLIATH

LIST THE POSSIBLE MASTER MATCHES

We previously created a list of players from our story of David and Goliath, and for the sake of brevity, I did the digging for details step on my own and included those details in the following chart. Now that our details are written out, it's time to start matching to the Master.

You may be thinking "I already know what the story of David and Goliath symbolizes. David is us, and Goliath is Satan and his temptations."

Yes, those are the typical comparisons we use when we talk about David and Goliath, and they're good ones. They teach us the great truth that there is no trial or temptation we'll face that is too great for us to conquer as long as we're on the Lord's side. It's a truth John affirmed when he wrote, "Ye are of God, little children, and have overcome . . . because greater is he that is in you, than he that is in the world" (1 John 4:4). Ammon likewise said, "I will boast of my God, for in his strength I can do all things" (Alma 26:12).

While knowing we "can do all things in Christ" (Philippians 4:13) is important, relating ourselves to David and Satan to Goliath is only one possible way of looking at the symbolism in the story. Even using that standard comparison, we've found a player that symbolizes ourselves and another that symbolizes Satan, but what symbolizes Christ? What more can we learn about our relationship with Him by either digging deeper or approaching the symbolism from a different angle?

Remember, we're not looking for "right" answers. We're looking for new insights into our relationship with Christ. Paul wrote that in Christ "are hid all the treasures of wisdom and knowledge" (Colossians 2:3). If we assume we already know what a story is about, it keeps us from digging deeper and finding the "hidden treasures" of knowledge the Lord has waiting for us (D&C 89:19).

So laying aside the comparisons we already know about this story, let's follow the steps of matching to the Master to see what else we can learn. Look through the following details and note any words or phrases that match what you know of Christ. You can make a list on a separate piece of paper, or you can circle, underline, or highlight the relevant phrases directly on these pages (though if this is a library book or you borrowed it from a friend, I wouldn't recommend the latter).

PLAYERS	DETAILS OF PLAYERS
Philistine army	Powerful, numerous, uncircumcised (didn't believe in God), want to destroy God's people Flee once fear set in
Israelite army	Afraid, insufficient faith, focused on worldly rewards for service Willing to pursue fleeing opponent
Standoff	Requires at least two opposing sides, often equally matched Waiting, tense, uncertain
Goliath	Enormous, intimidating, patient, persistent, mocking Champion of enemies, confident to the point of arrogance

PLAYERS	DETAILS OF PLAYERS
Goliath's armor	Brass, multiple pieces covering multiple body parts, heavy, protective but didn't protect everywhere
Goliath's challenge	Mocking, singling individual out from group, all-or-nothing stakes, relentless, repeated daily, makes a promise the Philistines didn't keep
David	Youngest brother, obedient, messenger for his father Prepared with scrip and sling Offended for God, focuses on spiritual consequence of not serving Faithful, courageous, previously prepared, acknowledges God's role in his preparation and success
Sheep	Livelihood for family, David's physical job Need a keeper, will be okay with various keepers
Bear and lion	Predators, threaten sheep, go after most vulnerable first Naturally stronger than a human, can hurt humans as well as sheep Killed by David
Jesse	David's dad, old man, tribe of Ephraim, lives in Bethlehem Has eight sons, cares about his sons, wants to keep them fed and in good standing with their commanders Owns sheep
Corn and loaves	For the brothers, provide physical aid, basic meal provided from their father
Ten cheeses	For the captain, gift to sustain leaders, more of a luxury food than bread
Keeper of sheep	Trusted, watches sheep in regular shepherd's absence

PLAYERS	DETAILS OF PLAYERS
King Saul	King, first doubtful, then believes on faith of others Willing to give his armor, unwilling or unable to fight himself
Saul's armor	Protects, multiple pieces, strong, high quality for king, requires some getting used to
David's staff	Helps keep balance on uneven terrain, provides support Long rod shape, might have had a shepherd's crook on it Probably wood, sturdy and reliable, can lean on it Used by David even when he isn't watching the sheep, something David always keeps on hand Could be used as weapon if needed, offense or defense
David's sling	Used for offense or defense, easily portable, requires practice to master Ineffective without stones, only as effective as person using it Works at a distance from enemy
Brook	Water, constantly flowing, not as big as a river, near battle, has stones in it
Stones	Five, smooth (because of brook), hard, relatively small in order to fit in sling Capable of wounding or killing things larger than it with right placement and force
The act of running to meet Goliath	No hesitancy or doubt, builds momentum, closes distance between enemy, gets stone within slinging range
The act of slinging a stone	Done by placing stone in sling, swinging in circles to build momentum, releasing one strap of sling at the right moment to let the stone fly Swinging requires speed to keep stone in the sling, release requires precision of timing to aim stone

What did you find? If your list looks different than mine, that's not a problem. We're all going to be guided by the Spirit to see things a little differently. Here are the attributes of Christ that the Spirit helped me find when I reviewed the details for the various players:

- Powerful (Philistine army)
- Patient, persistent (Goliath)
- Obedient, messenger for his father, offended for God, focuses on spiritual consequences, faithful, courageous, previously prepared, acknowledges God's role in his preparation and success (David)
- Cares about his sons, wants to keep them fed and in good standing (Jesse)
- Provides physical aid, provided from our Father (corn and loaves)
- Trusted, watches sheep in regular shepherd's absence (keeper of sheep)
- King, willing to give armor (King Saul)
- Protects, strong, requires some getting used to (Saul's armor)
- Helps keep balance, provides support, sturdy and reliable, can lean on it, useful outside of work, something to always keep close by, can provide offense or defense (David's staff)
- Constant (brook)
- No hesitancy or doubt (the act of running to meet Goliath)

PICK A MATCH FOR CHRIST

Once we've made our list, our next step is to pick one possible match and take it for a test drive to see how it feels as we ponder it further. If it feels right, we can keep exploring that mental path and see what other insights it inspires. If we start to ponder the match and it feels wrong, we can just move on to another possible match.

For example, Christ is "all-powerful" (Alma 44:5) and "the God of patience" (Romans 15:5), and when it comes to persistence, there is no end to the number of times or ways He reaches out to get our attention and bring us back to Him (D&C 43:25). Yet despite being powerful like the Philistine army and patient and persistent like Goliath, neither of those players feel like a good Christ-match to me. I just don't feel right comparing Christ to things that don't believe in God, want to destroy God's people, flee in fear, and mock others.

Not every characteristic or detail of a player has to match the thing we're comparing it to, but if most of the details are in direct opposition of the attributes of the thing we're trying to compare it with, it'll likely feel wrong. Trust those feelings. Trust the Spirit to guide you. Move on from that pairing and try something else.

Even though the Philistine army and Goliath have too many negative associations for me to feel comfortable moving forward with either of them as a match for Christ, considering those possible connections wasn't a waste of time by any means. It had me pondering Christ's power compared with Satan's power.

Sometimes we want to think Satan has nothing in common with Christ, but that's simply not true. They both had a plan of how to get Heavenly Father's children through mortality and back to His presence, and they are both powerful beings, including having the power to seal us to them, as we read in Mosiah and Alma: "Therefore, I would that ye should be steadfast and immovable, always abounding in good works, that Christ, the Lord God Omnipotent, may seal you his" (Mosiah 5:15). "For behold, if ye have procrastinated the day of your repentance even until death, behold, ye have become subjected to the spirit of the devil, and he doth seal you his" (Alma 34:35).

I'll admit, I don't like considering that Christ has attributes in common with Satan. It forces me to consider that if Christ, a perfect being, has things in common with him, how much more do I, an imperfect being, have in common with the adversary? But while it's not a pleasant truth to ponder, it is an important one because it can help me stay alert to my flaws and weaknesses and how Satan will patiently, persistently, and powerfully try to exploit them, like he did with the Nephites: "Now the cause of this iniquity of the people was this—Satan had great power, unto the stirring up of the people to do all manner of iniquity, and to the puffing them up with pride, tempting them to seek for power, and authority, and riches, and the vain things of the world" (3 Nephi 6:15).

By considering a match between Christ and either the Philistine army or Goliath, I ended up with a renewed commitment to try and be more like Christ and to be vigilant against the attacks of the adversary. I may not move forward with the Philistine army or Goliath as a symbolic match for Christ, but they provided an opportunity for me to ponder Christ and strengthen my testimony all the same.

We still need a player to match to Christ that we feel good moving forward with. The next player on my list of possible Master matches is David. According to our details list, David was obedient, a messenger for his father, offended for God, focused on spiritual consequences, faithful, courageous, and previously prepared. He also acknowledged God's role in his preparation and success. Those are eight very strong matching attributes David shares with Christ. I feel good moving forward with that pairing.

IF CHRIST IS HERE, WHERE AM I?

We often look at this story with David being an analog for ourselves, but if we re-examine it with David being a shadow of Christ, where would that put us in the story?

Let's look at King Saul. He was unwilling, or unable, to face and defeat Goliath himself. Are there trials or temptations that are too great for us to bear alone? King Saul also initially doubted David's ability before finally choosing to have faith in him. I don't know about you, but there are definitely times when my fear and doubt overpower my faith, and I need a little convincing to get back to a place where my faith conquers my fear. I think King Saul is a great choice to compare ourselves to if we consider David a representation of Christ.

Once we find a match for Christ and for ourselves, the next step is to ask questions about the relationship between those two players to help us better understand our relationship with Christ.

One question we might ask is why David went to Saul to ask his permission. David had the power to kill Goliath on his own;

he didn't need Saul's armor or weapons. He already knew what needed to be done and how to do it, so why didn't he just go get the stones and slay Goliath as soon as he heard him taunting the army and mocking God? Why bother going to the king first?

Because while there is no sin or sorrow you face that Christ can't heal and no Goliath He can't slay, He "hath given unto you that ye might choose" (Helaman 14:31). In other words, Christ will not force the saving power of His Atonement on you or anyone else.

Remember those verses about Christ and Satan both having the power to seal us to them? There's an important detail in those verses. Before either one can seal us to them, we have to exercise our own power. We choose to be steadfast, immovable, and abounding in good works, or we choose to procrastinate our repentance. We choose who we want to be sealed to. Their power, as mighty as it is, cannot override the power of our agency. As Alma the Younger taught his son Corianton, "Whosoever will come may come and partake of the waters of life freely; and whosoever will not come the same is not compelled to come" (Alma 42:27).

Yes, the gift of resurrection comes freely and automatically to us all, and we will be returned to God's presence to be judged (2 Nephi 9:10–15), but we are not guaranteed to stay in His presence. Those who are "filthy still . . . shall go away" (2 Nephi 9:16). Christ offers mercy and a chance to stay in God's presence, but justice demands we do our small part to show we want to take advantage of the mercy offered. It demands we give permission through specific choices we make.

Christ is continually seeking our permission to let Him be our Savior.

If we want Christ's Atonement to give us peace amidst our trials, we give our permission by having faith. "Therefore being justified by faith, we have peace with God through our Lord Jesus Christ" (Romans 5:1).

If we want Christ's Atonement to cleanse us from our sins, we give our permission by sincerely repenting. "According to justice, the plan of redemption could not be brought about, only on conditions of repentance. . . . Except it were for these conditions, mercy could not take effect" (Alma 42:13).

If we want Christ's Atonement to grant us eternal life, we give our permission by being baptized and receiving the Holy Ghost—by making and keeping covenants. "And now, as ye are desirous to . . . have eternal life . . . what have you against being baptized in the name of the Lord, as a witness before him that ye have entered into a covenant with him, that ye will serve him and keep his commandments, that he may pour out his Spirit more abundantly upon you?" (Mosiah 18:8–10).

Just as David sought Saul's permission to be Israel's champion, Christ is continually seeking our permission to let Him be our Savior. But while Saul did give his permission to David, it wasn't his immediate response. At first, he doubted David. As we notice that detail of their relationship, we might consider if there are ways in which we doubt Christ.

Are we doing anything in our lives that demonstrates to Christ we don't fully believe in His Atonement? Are there mistakes we've made or offenses others have committed against us that we believe (through our unwillingness to forgive ourselves or others) are too great for Christ's Atonement to pardon? Do we ever refuse to turn to Him in our sorrow or grief because deep down we don't think a pain as great as the one we're feeling can ever be healed?

We may believe in the power of Christ's Atonement, but do we believe it is truly infinite, that it is greater than any experience we may face in mortality?

Or do we believe in an Atonement with limitations?

MATCHING ADDITIONAL PLAYERS

As you ask questions about the relationship between the symbols you've selected for Christ and yourself, those questions are often answered by finding matches for additional players within the context of the Christ-and-you relationship you're already exploring.

For example, in examining Saul's initial doubt of David, we could also consider why he switched from doubt to faith. What changed his heart?

What previous victories has Christ had in your life?

Looking back at 1 Samuel 17:33–37, the only thing that happened between Saul saying "Thou art not able to go against this Philistine" and "Go, and the Lord be with thee" was David recounting the previous victories he'd had against the bear and the lion and testifying that God would give him victory now as He had back then.

If David used his victories with the bear and the lion to strengthen Saul's faith, then what could the bear and lion represent in your relationship with Christ? What previous victories has Christ had in your life?

Has He forgiven you before? Worked miracles in your life? Provided peace or comfort during turbulent times? How might remembering the ways He has proved Himself in the past help you trust more fully in His Atonement now?

REIMAGINE THE MATCHES

In considering Christ as David and us as King Saul, we've been able to ponder our beliefs on the power of the Atonement, ways Christ has blessed us in the past, and our role in letting Christ heal us (or seal us). We could absolutely stop there, having had a successful study and meditation.

With many subjects, though, there is more than one match for Christ, and for every Christ-match, there is often more than one match for ourselves. Some subjects may be rich enough to provide multiple days' worth of matching and pondering. So when you feel you've exhausted one set of matches, switch the players for either you or Christ and see what that new relationship can teach you.

For example, King Saul isn't the only possible match for us when we consider Christ as David. Just as David left his sheep in the care of someone else when he went off to do his work on the battlefront, Christ asked Peter to "feed my lambs" and "feed my sheep" when He left the kingdom in the apostles' hands after His Resurrection (John 21:15–17). What if instead of King Saul, we compared ourselves to the keeper of the sheep? The one no one even bothered to record by name? The one who stayed behind while everyone else was doing the more exciting and seemingly impressive jobs out on the battlefield? What could this new comparison teach us about our relationship with Christ?

Some of the ways God asks us to serve and minister in His kingdom feel unglamorous and often go unrecognized. (There are probably some ward librarians, nursery workers, and building cleaning coordinators adamantly nodding their heads right now.) For me, perhaps the calling that feels the most unglamorous is that of motherhood.

Don't get me wrong. Raising children of God to have faith in Him and make and keep sacred covenants is an eternally important labor of love and an opportunity I'm so grateful to have. But there are definitely parts of my maternal calling that feel much more like labor than love.

Planning a menu, going grocery shopping, preparing meals, and washing the dishes day after day, and week after week, with no end in sight is tedious and exhausting. While those things are not an essential part of motherhood (you can still be a great mother even if you hire cooks and housekeepers), they are necessary household tasks and—at least in my home—are a big part of my responsibility as a mother. And what kind of recognition do I get for the endless hours I spend trying to keep a steady flow of nutritious yet kid-friendly meals on the table?

The sweet voice of one of my beloved children saying "I don't like this" before we've even blessed the food.

Motherhood has also seen me sporting milk-soaked bras, making up songs to help a toddler through a bout of constipation, and instinctually catching my child's vomit in my bare hands to try and protect their shoes and the carpet.

Despite all the joy that motherhood brings into my life, the lack of glamour and recognition is hard at times. But when I consider the unnamed keeper of the sheep that David trusted in his absence, it helps me remember that God is trusting me and that He knows the work I'm doing, even if no one else does. It helps me realize, like Alma the Younger did, that instead of wishing God had entrusted me with other duties, "I ought to be content with the things which the Lord hath allotted unto me" (Alma 29:3).

When I consider myself as a keeper of the sheep, it makes me want to live up to His trust by caring for His children in whichever way He asks, even if it doesn't come with any glory or recognition at all.

(RE)REIMAGINE THE MATCHES

We've considered Christ as David, and us as both King Saul and the keeper of the sheep. What if we went with the more familiar comparison where David symbolizes us, and Goliath represents Satan? Where might Christ be in that comparison?

It's only through Christ that we defeat Satan, so Christ could be the stones that David used to defeat Goliath. Easy peasy, right?

Sure. But what new insights does that give us? What do we learn about our relationship to Christ through that comparison? Let's dig deeper by considering a few questions about David's relationship to the stones:

- Where did David find the stones?
- How did he know they would be there?
- Why didn't he grab whatever stones were surely closer at hand?
- Why did he choose five when he only needed one?
- How did David use the stones?

To me, the first three questions are all related. David needed the stones to be smooth, or they wouldn't fly true. That's why he couldn't grab whatever rocks were nearest to him; those stones would be rough, and thus, ineffective. He went to the brook to select his stones because he knew the constant flow of the brook would've smoothed out the edges of the stones. He might never have been to this brook before, but he knew that flowing water worked the same everywhere. If he had gotten smooth stones to practice with from the brook at home, he could rely on the brook near the battle site to provide the same.

There is only one source of salvation that is true and effective, and it is Christ.

Likewise, we can't find salvation in whatever worldly offerings surround us. There is only one source of salvation that is true and effective, and it is Christ. Only He can save us, because only He has been smoothed and perfected by His sinless life and His suffering in Gethsemane and on Calvary. Only He has "descended below all things" (D&C 88:6). Only He is the "tried stone" that Isaiah deemed a "sure foundation" (Isaiah 28:16).

Just as David knew where to find smooth stones at home and at the battlefield, we too can confidently find Christ anywhere we go. He has told us where to find Him—in His Church, in His temple, in His holy word. I've traveled to and lived in many states and countries, and anywhere I've attended sacrament meeting, no matter what language the meeting is in, the covenants I renew are the same. What a blessing that is.

As for the last two questions, I think they're related as well. David obviously had sufficient faith in God to help him defeat Goliath and defeating him only took one stone, so why did David take five? I think it was because while his faith in God's abilities was great, so was his humility. He knew that his own abilities played a part. He had to sling the stone at precisely the right time, with the precise speed and direction as well. He had practiced before, and he carried his sling with him as a way of life, but David knew he wasn't perfect. He acknowledged that despite all his practice and previous success, he might make mistakes. But he also had enough faith that if his first stone didn't land right, God would keep him safe until he had a chance to sling the second, third, fourth, and fifth.

Have we, like David, practiced using Christ's Atonement to the point we feel proficient at it? Do we repent daily as a way of life? Do we know how to tap into the power of His Atonement for more than just forgiveness?

I remember one Relief Society lesson where a beloved convert friend of mine courageously raised her hand during a lesson and asked the teacher, "You mentioned drawing upon the strength of Christ's Atonement, but I don't understand. How do you actually do that?"

Thanks to countless Primary and family home evening lessons, I could break down repentance into a wonderfully alliterative, step-by-step process.

1. Recognize the wrong.
2. Request forgiveness from all parties, including God.
3. Restore or repair the damage as best you can.
4. Resolve to never do it again.

Until my friend asked her question, however, I'd never had a lesson that gave detailed instructions for the process of drawing upon Christ's Atonement for comfort and strength.

The sisters in the room took turns offering their own insights as to how they personally drew upon Christ's Atonement. Some mentioned prayer, others scripture study, and others suggested meditation and giving service. That lesson helped me realize how much practice and personal experience goes into fully utilizing Christ's Atonement. It is definitely a learned skill.

As we learn to apply Christ's Atonement in our lives, we'll make mistakes, not just sins (though surely, we'll have those as well). There may be times we won't let ourselves be comforted or times we let our fear get the best of us. Some of our personal Goliaths may go down on the first shot; others may take us a while to defeat. The good news is, we get as many shots as we need to get it right, as long as we're humble enough to keep launching stones.

MY FATHER DWELT IN A TENT

SELECT THE SUBJECT

For our last guided example, we're going to take the Christ-finding process from start to finish using the scripture 1 Nephi 2:15 as our subject.

"*And my father dwelt in a tent.*"

That's it. That's the whole verse.

As a youth, my friends and I often laughed about how such a random, silly detail was not only mentioned but had its own seven-word verse all to itself.

I no longer laugh at this verse. When I first broke down my mental Christ-finding process into various steps, I challenged myself to make sure it really could work for any subject. I tested it on this verse, and what followed was one of the best scripture study sessions I have had.

When selecting a subject that is simple or short, we want to ask questions to flesh it out and consider the context in which that subject occurs.

Questions we might ask for the simple situation of "my father dwelt in a tent" include:

- What happened before he lived in the tent?
- Where was Lehi's tent?
- Why was he there?
- Was anyone else with him?

148

We could ask other questions and get as detailed as we want with our answers, but for my scripture study, these are the questions I used and the answers I came up with:

SUBJECT	"MY FATHER DWELT IN A TENT" (1 NEPHI 2:15)
What happened before he lived in the tent?	Lehi lived in Jerusalem with his family; they had a comfortable life with lots of worldly goods Lehi preached repentance but was rejected
Where was Lehi's tent?	The wilderness between Jerusalem and the promised land
Why was he there?	He had a revelation where God commanded him to take his family, leave Jerusalem, and move to the promised land
Was anyone else with him?	His family, which later included Zoram and Ishmael's family

PICK THE PLAYERS

Once we've selected and sufficiently fleshed out a subject, the next step in the Christ-finding process is to pull out all the nouns and list them as our players. Remember that verbs can become nouns by adding the phrase "the act of" before them. Also, if some of the nouns feel too similar, we can combine them into the same player, as directed by the Spirit. We can also combine or split them later in the process if we feel it's necessary at that point.

Here are the players I pulled from my previous answers.

PLAYERS INVOLVED WITH 1 NEPHI 2:15
Lehi
Tent
Jerusalem
Lehi's family
Comfortable life and worldly goods
The act of preaching
The act of being rejected
Wilderness
Promised land
Revelation/commandment

The questions I used and answers I provided don't cover everything in the story of Lehi's family in the wilderness; they don't mention going back for the brass plates, the Liahona, the broken bows, the lack of fires and subsequent need to eat things raw, building the ships, etc. And that's okay. What we've listed so far is enough to get us started.

If you ever feel like you don't have enough players to work with, you can always go back and flesh out your subject even further to give yourself more players. How much to expand a subject and how many players to start with is a decision only you and the Spirit can make together. The more players you start with, the more you'll have to work with later, but remember not to let yourself get overwhelmed. Good enough is good enough.

DIG FOR DETAILS

Once we have our list of players, it's time to record details about each of our players. Adjectives, functions, definitions, relationships with other players—anything that comes to mind goes in the detail section.

If you feel like you don't know what to write, that's a good time to do some research in dictionaries, online articles, other scriptures discussing the topic, etc. For me, when I got to the player Jerusalem, I did some additional research and found some nicknames and descriptions of the city I hadn't known, such as how Lamentations 2:15 refers to it as "perfection of beauty."

If you have time to dig deep for details through research, you can find some hidden gems of knowledge. If you don't have time, simply write details using what you already know and trust the Spirit to help it be enough.

Here are the details I came up with for our list of players.

PLAYERS IN 1 NEPHI 2:15	DETAILS OF PLAYERS
Lehi	Obedient to God
	Father, leader, spiritually powerful
	Rejected, others sought to kill him
Tent	Humble abode compared to previous home
	Temporary shelter, portable, likely not as comfortable
	Lots of work taking it down and putting it up all the time
Jerusalem	Holy City, City of Peace, "perfection of beauty"
	Temple was there (eventually destroyed)
	Had some righteous citizens who were commanded to leave and lots of other citizens who stayed and were taken captive
Lehi's family	Followed him to wilderness
	Included in-laws such as Ishmael's family and Zoram
	Varying levels of obedience and testimony
	Lehi loved them all, even those who rejected him and his teachings and wanted to go back
Comfortable life and worldly goods	Desirable, provide comfort and ease
	Left behind in Jerusalem
	Used to try and buy the brass plates

PLAYERS IN 1 NEPHI 2:15	DETAILS OF PLAYERS
The act of preaching	Commanded to do it
	Takes courage, especially preaching to those who don t want to hear what you're saying
	God supports you when you do it
The act of being rejected	Discouraging, dangerous if the rejection turns violent
	Happened with strangers before wilderness and his own sons during wilderness
Wilderness	Rough conditions, physically hard, full of trials, uncivilized, natural
	Necessary point on journey, not final destination
Promised land	Requires journey to reach, desirable place to live, lots of blessings
	No pictures or descriptions of its details were given beforehand, just a promise that it would be wonderful
Revelation/ commandment	From God, unable to get from man
	Must be received and obeyed to reap blessings, affects others as well
	Happened both before wilderness and in wilderness

MATCH TO THE MASTER

Now that we've got our players and details, it's time to read over the list of details and look for any that relate to Christ. You can make a list of all the possible matches, but if one jumps out at you right away and you know you want to explore it more, it's okay to forego making a list of all the possibilities and instead dive into the match you've already found.

During my initial study of this verse, Lehi stood out to me as a match for Christ so strongly, I didn't want to bother looking for others. Every single attribute I listed for Lehi could be said of the Savior as well:

- Obedient: Christ was obedient to God when He said in Gethsemane, "Nevertheless not as I will, but as thou wilt" (Matthew 26:39).

- Father: He is a father because our covenants make us "the children of Christ, his sons, and his daughters" (Mosiah 5:7).

- Leader: He is a leader to those who "forsook all, and followed him" (Luke 5:11).

- Spiritually powerful: Christ is so spiritually powerful that "even the wind and sea obey him" (Mark 4:41).

- Rejected: Christ was also "rejected of men" (Isaiah 53:3).

- Others sought to kill him: "Jesus walked in Galilee: for he would not walk in Jewry, because the Jews sought to kill him" (John 7:1).

IF CHRIST IS HERE, WHERE AM I?

Now that we've matched a player in our subject to the Savior, we want to figure out where we are in that subject in relationship to the Savior. So if Lehi is a type for the Savior, then who are we? Remember, this process might take some trial and error to find a match that feels right to you, and you may find more than one match that feels right. Each match you ponder and explore will help you learn more about your relationship with Christ, and that is the only objective we have with this Christ-finding exercise.

> **Pondering your relationship with Christ is the only objective.**

One possible match for us that comes to my mind is Jerusalem. Just as it was designed to be holy and beautiful, we too have a divine nature and beautiful infinite worth. Jerusalem had both righteous and wicked citizens in it, and most of us have some righteousness and some wickedness in us as well. But since we're not trying to simply match attributes between ourselves and any of the players, we need to consider what the relationship was between Lehi (the match for Christ) and Jerusalem (the player we're pondering as a match for us).

Lehi chose Jerusalem as the place to raise his family, and he probably loved it. Yet, he had to give up on it and leave it behind. With all we know about the Savior and "his patience, and his long-suffering toward the children of men" (Mosiah 4:6), does that feel like an accurate parallel to our relationship with Christ?

At first, it didn't to me. The idea of Christ leaving me and abandoning me didn't feel right, so I moved on to finding another match for myself.

As I write this chapter, though, years after my initial Christ-finding scripture study session with this passage, the Spirit is inspiring me with ideas of the Final Judgment and how justice will demand that Christ leaves us to face the consequences of our own sins if we refuse to follow Him. Because, as He said, "if they would not repent they must suffer even as I" (D&C 19:17). There's truth there. It wasn't the truth I needed years ago, back when I was first finding myself in the Lehi story, but it is definitely giving me something to ponder right now.

Another possible match for ourselves, and the one I settled on during my initial study, is that of Lehi's family. Similar to Jerusalem, Lehi's family displayed varying levels of obedience and testimony. But instead of being left behind like Jerusalem was, the family followed Lehi. Even Laman and Lemuel, who we often associate solely with doubt and disobedience, followed their dad into the wilderness. They went back to Jerusalem for the plates and again for Ishmael's family, and each time they returned to the wilderness despite how much they wanted to stay in their familiar former home. I'd like to think that even in my most Laman-esque moments of grumbling and complaining, I'm still willing to follow Christ like Laman and Lemuel (at least initially) followed their dad.

MATCHING ADDITIONAL PLAYERS

Once you've found both yourself and Christ, you can stop if you need to or if you're satisfied with the things you've learned and pondered about your relationship with Him. If you want to ponder even more, however, the next step is to find matches for additional players within the context of the matches you already have.

Consider Jerusalem, a holy place of peace and beauty, a place where Lehi was comfortable and rich but had to leave if he wanted to obey God. How does that relate to Christ? Was there a place of beauty and perfection where Christ was rich and comfortable, but He obediently left it behind when God told Him to?

Doesn't that sound a lot like heaven? "For I came down from heaven," Christ said, "not to do mine own will, but the will of him that sent me" (John 6:38).

Not every player needs to fit into the analogy you make, but if Lehi represents Christ, Lehi's family represents us, and Jerusalem represents heaven, so many of the other players in this subject start to fall into place. The wilderness can represent mortality, and the promised land can represent our celestial glory awaiting us in heaven. Just as Lehi guided his family through the wilderness to see them safely to the promised land, Christ and His gospel guide us through mortality to help us reach our eternal destiny.

And what about the main focus of our original verse in question—the tent?

Nephi was used to seeing his father living comfortably in their home. Now he saw this man of exceedingly great wealth (see 1 Nephi 3:22–25) willingly reduced to living in a tent in the wilderness. I imagine that Nephi would have been so struck by the contrast that he couldn't help but record it. There are probably lots of other details Nephi could have included to highlight this contrast, but he chose the tent—which showcases not only the humble nature of Lehi's new lifestyle, but also its nomadic nature. There was no permanent spot for the tent, no permanent home.

Despite being "highly exalted" by God, Christ "made himself of no reputation" when He came to earth (Philippians 2:7–9). He left the glories of heaven not just for a mortal existence, but for a *humble* mortal existence, one in which He "ha[d] not where to lay his head" (Matthew 8:20).

Before I took the time to write out all the players and details surrounding 1 Nephi 2:15, I assumed it was simply a funny little sidenote from Nephi that had the honor of being the shortest verse in the Book of Mormon. After following the Christ-finding process, however, the simple statement that Lehi dwelt in a tent transformed into a poignant reminder of the glories and riches in heaven Christ chose to leave behind when He descended to earth and lived in the humblest of circumstances, all so He could safely guide the people He loves, including me and you, through the wilderness of mortality.

REIMAGINE THE MATCHES

If you want to keep exploring a subject for additional insights, try substituting a different player as a match for Christ and/or yourself. What if we were to use Lehi as a symbol for us instead of Christ? I believe most of us are doing our best to obey God, even when it requires sacrifice. We all have people we love who we're trying to help along their journeys while we do our best to be righteous and stay spiritually strong. Therefore, Lehi is also a good symbol for us.

Our next step in this reimagining would be to find a player to symbolize Christ in comparison with ourselves as Lehi. To do this, we would look at the list of details and keep in mind the relationship between players.

One player that stands out to me as representative of Christ is the tent. Just as a tent provides shelter, Isaiah taught that Christ is "a refuge from the storm, a shadow from the heat" (Isaiah 25:4).

Feeling stuck? Try rephrasing some details or adding players that are implied.

Now that we have both matches, we can ask, "If we are Lehi and Christ is the tent, what does that teach us about our relationship with Christ?"

Lehi "left his house, and the land of his inheritance, and his gold, and his silver, and his precious things, and took nothing with him, save it were his family, and provisions, and tents, and departed into the wilderness" (1 Nephi 2:4). He only took the essentials, and the tent was one of those.

From that, we can learn that Christ is essential to our spiritual survival and that we don't need all the other precious things of life if we understand what "the precious blood of Christ" being shed for us truly means (1 Peter 1:19). We can also learn that we are meant to dwell in Christ. How do we dwell in Him? Through making and continually renewing our covenants with Him. "He that eateth my flesh, and drinketh my blood, dwelleth in me, and I in him" (John 6:56).

If reading through your details list doesn't spark any ideas, rephrasing some of them can help. Just as we did with our hand-crank flashlight, we could rephrase "portable" as "able to go with us anywhere." We could also rephrase "wanted to go back" as "wanted comfort or familiarity" since those were key reasons why Laman and Lemuel wanted to return to Jerusalem.

Another tip if you feel stuck is to think of players that might be implied but aren't explicitly written on your list yet. For example, we put revelation on our list of players, but we never listed who the revelation came from. Lehi was given revelation and spiritual power from God, so another player we could add is God (which makes for an obvious match to Christ).

If we are Lehi and Christ is God/Himself, what can that relationship teach us? As we examine the interactions between Lehi and God, we see that God gave Lehi revelation while he lived in Jerusalem as a wealthy man of status (1 Nephi 2:1–2), as well as when he was in the wilderness, dwelling in a tent (1 Nephi 2:14). If we plug ourselves into the story in place of Lehi, we learn that God doesn't care if we are wealthy or poor. No matter what our worldly station is, He will bless us with revelation and spiritual power as long as we are obedient.

We've considered Christ as Lehi, a tent, and God/Himself. We've considered ourselves as Lehi's family and Lehi. None of those matches are better or worse than the others; they're all simply different. The Spirit can use each one to add new layers to our understanding so we can know not only where Christ is and where we are, but more importantly, how we can draw closer to Him so that we can "abide in him; that, when he shall appear, we may have confidence" (1 John 2:28).

We don't need all the other precious things of life if we understand what the precious blood of Christ being shed for us truly means.

CONCLUSION

I hope no matter how capable you previously felt when it came to finding symbols of Christ, you now feel empowered to search for Him in new ways. I also hope you feel increasingly confident in His promise that you will find Him whenever and wherever you seek Him.

I'll leave you with a blank template you can photocopy to use as many times as you need, along with some ideas of things you can practice finding Christ in. But before I do, I want to quickly talk about feasts. We opened this book with a story about food; it seems only fitting we should close with one.

My grandpa, John H. Groberg, has served in many capacities as a member of the Church, but his time spent living in Tonga and Hawaii as well as traveling to so many of the island nations of the Pacific has given him a special bond with the Polynesian Saints. They call him Kolipoki, and it has always amazed me to see the love they have for him, even here in the United States.

When I was a newlywed in California in 2007, my grandpa came to visit. The Rancho Cucamonga Stake (which included a Tongan ward) was celebrating the 20th anniversary of when it had been organized, and to celebrate, they held a luau. My grandpa had helped organize the stake, so he was invited back for the luau as a guest of honor. He invited my husband Dustin and me to attend with him and my grandma. It was my first true Polynesian feast, and while I knew there would be a lot of good food, I was still completely blown away by what awaited us on the table.

There was a roast pig, beautiful fruit arrangements, and more side dishes than I can remember or count, even with the help of the photo. The food was piled high, and everything you see in this photo was for just the four of us. Each long table in our row had four people at it, and each table held a similar mountain of delicious offerings. It was, in every sense of the word, a feast.

Feasting is more than eating a lot of food, however. Feasting is almost always in celebration of something. The word *feast* comes from the Latin word *festus*, meaning joyous, and it is not meant to be a solo activity. Feasting is a communal effort. Many hands go into preparing the food, and many people are meant to eat it.

At the luau, the four of us barely made a dent in our portion of the meal as we watched the dancers and other performers on the stage in front of us. I was a little worried about what would happen with all the uneaten food, but my worries were unnecessary (as they almost always are). As we left our seats, members of the stake that had been helping run the event came to the tables from all sides and took their turns eating. Within a matter of minutes, all the food was consumed. It made me happy not

only to see that the food didn't go to waste, but that so many others were able to enjoy the food as we had.

In the parable of the great supper, a certain man prepares a feast and invites his friends, but they reject the invitation. There is no joy or celebration in eating a feast alone, so the man sends his servant to invite the poor and injured to his home to feast with him instead. They come, and then my favorite part of the parable happens:

"And the servant said, Lord, it is done as thou hast commanded, and yet there is room. And the lord said unto the servant, Go out into the highways and hedges, and compel them to come in, that my house may be filled" (Luke 14:22–23).

It wasn't enough for the man to have some people to celebrate with. He wanted *everyone* to come feast—he wanted his house filled. Why? Because "if your joy will be great with one soul that you have brought unto me into the kingdom of my

Father, how great will be your joy if you should bring many souls unto me!" (D&C 18:16). There is gospel truth in the adage "the more, the merrier."

So what do these ideas of feasting and communal joy have to do with our process of finding symbols of Christ around us? In the Book of Mormon, we're commanded to "feast upon the words of Christ" (2 Nephi 32:3) and "feast upon his love" (Jacob 3:2). We can partake of the words of Christ and feel His love by ourselves, but if we want to *feast* on those things, we need each other because true feasting requires community.

In an effort to help us feast together on Christ's words and His love, I've created a Facebook group called "Finding Christ in Your Daily Life." I would love to have you join our community there and share the symbols of Christ you've found or any insights you have. If you'd rather share them with just me instead of a public group (or if you have any questions at all), please email me at FindingChrist@whitneyhemsath.com.

Finding Christ on our own is wonderful. Finding Him together is an even greater joy. But no matter how, when, or with whom we go looking for Him, His promise remains the same: "Draw near unto me and I will draw near unto you; seek me diligently and ye shall find me; ask, and ye shall receive; knock, and it shall be opened unto you" (D&C 88:63).

Hold to that promise and remember that your efforts are always enough when they're guided by the Spirit.

See you at the feast!

Whitney

APPENDIX

THE CHRIST-FINDING PROCESS AT A GLANCE

- **Take the Time:** Be intentional about practicing your Christ-finding skills. Find whatever time, schedule, or triggers work for you, but be consistent so you can truly build a habit.

- **Write and Record:** It's not required, but whenever possible, write your thoughts as you work through the process.

- **Select the Subject:** Anything counts as a subject. Ask yourself questions to expand the subject if necessary.

- **Pick the Players:** Make note of the nouns involved in your subject, including "the act of *verb*ing."

- **Dig for Details:** Come up with as many details for each player as you can. Adjectives, adverbs, relationships, functions, definitions, etc.

- **Match to the Master:** Search your list of details for any that match what you know of Christ. Once you've found Him, find where you are in relationship to Him. What can the other players represent, and what might those symbols teach you about your relationship with Christ? If you have time, try reimagining some of the matches.

- **Forward with Faith:** There are no right answers. There's just you being guided by the Spirit, seeking Christ the best you can with the promise that as you seek, so shall you find.

POTENTIAL SUBJECTS FOR FINDING CHRIST

SINGLE OBJECTS	SIMPLE SITUATIONS	COMPLETE STORIES
Podium	Washing windows	Something that happened on your last vacation
Sauerkraut	Toasting bread	
Sunscreen	Switching out summer clothes for winter ones	A time you built something
Headphones		
Oil change	Backing up documents to the cloud	How you celebrated your last birthday
Velcro		
Fire hydrant	Folding laundry only to find you're missing a sock	The last thing you did with one of your parents
Nachos		
Storage ottoman	Making s'mores	Something you saw happen at the grocery store
Rollercoaster		
Paperclip	Running a marathon	A time you won something
Crosswalk	Learning to drive	
Piñata	Checking the mail	The scariest moment you've ever had
Earplugs		
Double-decker bus	Folding a fitted sheet	Judges 3:12–30 (Ehud the assassin)
Baby monitor	Picking wildflowers	
Photocopy machine	Giving a talk at church	2 Samuel 21:15–22 (David and the four sons of Goliath)
Pencil sharpener		

SINGLE OBJECTS (CONT.)

Boa constrictor

Yo-yo

Bookmark

Picture frame

Balloon

Avalanche

Dice

Elephant

Dryer sheet

Jumper cables

Arcade games

Windshield

Plunger

Spiral-bound notebook

Hotel

Hair tie

Tweezers

Microscope

SIMPLE SITUATIONS (CONT.)

Walking a dog

Getting a bad haircut

A tree shedding leaves in the fall

Breaking in a new pair of shoes

Hemming a pair of pants

Changing a light bulb

Renewing books from the library

Cleaning out your email inbox

Hard-boiling an egg

Painting with watercolors

Having a garage sale

Forgetting to take the trash to the curb

COMPLETE STORIES (CONT.)

2 Kings 6:1–7 (Elisha and the axe)

John 12:9–11 (Lazarus's enemies)

John 20:1–10 (John and Peter race to the empty tomb)

Acts 5:1–11 (Ananias and Sapphira lie to Peter)

Acts 12:1–17 (Peter is rescued from prison and Rhoda tells others about it)

For more subject ideas, visit Whitney's website.

QUESTIONS FOR
FLESHING OUT A SUBJECT

SINGLE OBJECTS

Who uses the object?

When or where would they use this object?

What is it used for?

How is it used?

What materials or components is the object made of?

SIMPLE SITUATIONS

Is this situation normal? If not, what does normal look like?

What events lead up to this situation?

What events follow this situation?

Who or what does this situation affect?

Is this situation (and/or its effects) desirable? If so, how is it brought about? If not desirable, how can it be avoided? In either case, are there obstacles that must be overcome?

How often does this situation occur?

What objects would be used to get into or out of this situation?

COMPLETE STORIES

What happened just before the story?

Were any events going on behind the scenes while the story unfolded that made the story possible?

QUESTIONS TO ASK WHEN DIGGING FOR DETAILS

What are the adjectives and adverbs associated with the nouns and verbs listed as players?

What does the player do or what is it used for?

What is the relationship between this player and the other players?

Are there any conditional aspects or requirements for the player to function?

Why was this word used and not a different one? What characteristics make this object or word different than other similar ones that might have been used instead?

Is this detail an essential characteristic of this player? Why is it essential? How is this characteristic created?

Is there any aspect of its definition you weren't aware of?

FINDING CHRIST TEMPLATE SHEET

Subject: _____

_____

_____

_____

_____

PLAYERS	DETAILS

POSSIBLE CHRIST MATCHES:

-
-
-
-
-

If Christ is _____ ,

then I could be _____ .

What might other players symbolize in this comparison?
What does this teach me about my relationship with Christ?

_____

_____

_____

_____

_____

_____

_____

_____

_____

_____

_____

Join us on Facebook in the
"Finding Christ in Your Daily Life" group.

Or email your questions and discoveries to
FindingChrist@WhitneyHemsath.com.

ACKNOWLEDGEMENTS

So many people have helped me over the years to bring this book into existence. I cannot possibly name them all, but I would feel ungrateful not to mention a few.

Kristen Gardner—One Sunday after one of my lessons, you approached me and said I should write a book about my gospel insights. I was probably too bashful to tell you at the time, but I went home that day and started crafting a few ideas. This book is the result. Thank you for giving me that spark of encouragement so many years ago.

My dear Summiteers Jana King, Kyra Palmer, and Loury Trader—Thank you for your feedback and ideas on the earliest draft of this book. Your encouragement was invaluable, as is your friendship.

David Fallon, Jake Fluekiger, and Jeanna Stay—While I never brought the main text of this project to our writing group, your support for my writing in general is such a boon.

And without you, I'd probably still be trying to decide between author photos and cover colors. Thank you for being my sounding board and for making writing group awesome. Seeing your lovely digitized faces is one of the highlights of my week. When I say that I love you all, I truly meme it. ;-)

Deanna Young—From our first flash fiction swap to our sci-fi fairytales, our dark mermaid stories to our latest unconventional epistolary ones, collaborating with you over the years has been a joy. You might not have been too involved with the text of this book, but your support and commiseration for so many aspects of my writing journey are a big reason I am where I am today. If I'm ever doubting myself as a writer, you have always been there to restore my faith in myself. Your friendship means all the worlds with all their moons to me.

Andrea Jarrett—After some discouraging consultations with publishers, I had set this project aside. Your offer to read and edit it, and all your subsequent encouraging remarks, rekindled my motivation and helped me refocus my efforts and hone this into the book it is. Thank you.

Krista Isaacson—Ever since I met you at my first writing conference, your support, beta reading, and mentoring in general have made all the difference on my path to publication. Thank you, friend. For cheering me on and for believing in this book's mission and potential despite my lack of marketable fame.

My wonderful beta readers Leanne M., Rae N., Coriel S., April G., Heidi S., Amy K.—Like a small brook smoothing out stones, you have helped remove the rougher edges of this manuscript. Thank you for your time and feedback.

Jeanna Stay—My magnificent editor, writing partner, and friend. You get double mentioned because you are simply that awesome. Thank you for lending your brilliant editing brain to this manuscript and answering so many questions about commas and quotation marks. You are a treasure, and if I were a bowerbird, I would collect you.

Emily Strong Rogers—Thank you for making this book beautiful, inside and out. For years, I have dreamed of this book with its cover and layout. You brought that dream to life, and it's so much better than I ever imagined. I feel honored to have worked with you.

Mom and Dad—Thank you for your faith and testimonies and for taking the time to have family home evening, go to church, and say family prayers. Your love is the foundation all my talents and confidence are built on. My whole life has been a feast because of you. Thank you for feasting with me.

My darling boys Jason, Evan, Clark, and Zac—Thank you for your patience with me as dinner was late some nights or when I had to skip a board game or two in order to meet a writing deadline. I hope watching me chase my dreams inspires you to do the same, and more than anything, I hope you seek Christ every single day and find yourself closer and closer to Him as you travel though life. I love you as perfectly as my imperfections allow and want you to know that being your mother has been and always will be one of the greatest privileges of my life.

Dustin—I could never have done this without your belief in me and the importance of this message. Your support has come through words of encouragement, patience and understanding when I sacrificed time together to be writing instead, holding down the fort so I could go to conferences and retreats, working hard to provide for our family so I have the privilege to pursue dreams like this, consoling me through bouts of tearful discouragement along the way, praising my gifts both to me and to others, and above all, your rock-solid testimony and love of our Savior that inspires me daily. I will love you forever, for always, and no matter what.

ABOUT THE AUTHOR

Whitney Owens Hemsath is an author of LDS inspirational nonfiction and poetry (who also writes fiction under the name W. O. Hemsath). She currently lives in Utah with her husband and four sons. When she's not writing, she enjoys doing cardio dance and eating frozen BYU mint brownies. She is a dynamic teacher and presenter, and details about her writing or how to book her for speaking engagements can be found at whitneyhemsath.com.

Photo Credit: Evelyn Hornbarger.

www.ingramcontent.com/pod-product-compliance
Lightning Source LLC
Chambersburg PA
CBHW061156120626
46546CB00005B/2086

* 9 7 8 1 9 6 3 6 5 9 0 0 9 *